Teach with Style

A Comprehensive System for Teaching Adults

Jim Teeters

Redleaf Press

St. Paul

Published by Redleaf Press
    a division of Resources for Child Caring
    450 N. Syndicate, Suite 5
    St. Paul, MN 55104

Distributed by Gryphon House
    Mailing Address:
    P.O. Box 207
    Beltsville, MD 20704-0207

Library of Congress Cataloging-in-Publication Data

Teeters, Jim, 1938–
    Teach with style : a comprehensive system for teaching adults / by Jim Teeters.
          p. cm.
    Includes bibliographical references.
    ISBN 1-929610-05-X
    1. Adult learning—Handbooks, manuals, etc. 2. Adult education—Handbooks, manuals, etc. I.
Title.

LC5225.L42 T44 2001
374'.1102—dc21

2001019179

To my mother, a writer

Contents

In appreciation

I appreciate all of the wonderful participants who have attended my workshops and classes over the years. They have taught me how to teach.

I appreciate the guidance and support of my colleagues, teaching partners, and friends who believed in me and in my approach to adult instruction.

Finally, I appreciate the patience of my editor, Jeanne Engelmann, who took on the difficult task of guiding me through the process of writing, and endured numerous bouts of rewriting.

Introduction

Are you an experienced adult instructor, or are you just beginning to teach and lead workshops? Do you teach short courses and workshops, or classes that extend over a period of weeks and months? Do you teach at a child care center or at a training conference center? Are you filled with confidence at your teaching assignment, or are you scared to death to face a group of people who may demand too much of you?

Well, I have good news for you. The concepts and tools in *Teach with Style* can help you teach better no matter what the setting or how experienced you are. This model applies to any teaching situation, whether it's a seminar, a parenting class, an employee training session, or coaching a new worker. The model includes four simple instructor styles with strategies and learning activities to help you teach effectively—that is, your adult students will learn and apply what you teach.

Whether experienced or new, instructors of adults can be rigid in their approach to teaching. Usually we keep abreast of our particular area of interest, but we may stagnate in the way we teach it. What keeps us growing, changing, and progressing? We need to see ourselves accurately through the eyes of our students and colleagues, and we need a clear method to examine and improve our practice. You will find *Teach with Style* the perfect guide for this process. Conscientiously followed, this simple program ensures positive results using an approach that your adult students will truly enjoy.

Child versus adult learners

One drizzly Sunday afternoon in Seattle I sipped coffee and gazed out a bakery window while a young mother zipped past, pushing her toddler in a stroller. With wide sparkling eyes the child greeted this common, everyday street scene as if it were a garden of delights. He seemed to be shouting, "Show me everything! I want it all!" If all adult students came to my workshops and classes with that same attitude, how easy it would be to teach. How differently adults and children approach new learning.

Eagerly and without reserve, the child in the stroller embraced his new, changing world and viewed even common things with a sense of wonder.

Young children approach learning with a singular focus. Their "show me" is straightforward and open, and they want to absorb each moment. When you teach something to young children, you do not need to prove its value. They just jump in and learn it.

Most adult students have quite a different attitude toward learning new things. When adult learners say "Show me!" they are often admonishing the instructor to make learning really count for something. Adults hope that their time is well spent, because time spent on learning competes with the more immediate demands of life.

The unspoken demands of busy adult learners are

- *Show me* why I should learn what you have to teach.
- *Show me* that you are knowledgeable and worthy of my time and attention.
- *Show me* that you can hold my interest so I will not get bored.
- *Show me* that you care enough to teach me what I want and need to learn.

Instructors are challenged to make their instruction meet the real needs of adult students and clearly demonstrate the benefits of committing time to a seminar, class, or conference.

The complexity of adult learners

One might think adults would be easy to teach because they are responsible and well behaved; on the contrary, I have found that adults present a formidable challenge. Adults add greater complexity to the classroom than young children do because adults consciously or unconsciously evaluate the instructor and the learning. This demands a deeper level of awareness on the part of the instructor. You must balance your attention between how you teach, what you teach, and how your adult students receive it.

Adults' expectations and anticipation of the learning experience contribute to this complexity. As soon as adults hear about your workshop or class, they begin to develop expectations about it. They anticipate it with various degrees of hope or fear because adults have a longer history of dealing with learning experiences, some of them pleasant and some painful. While they learn, adults also evaluate you and your promises to them in light of what they experience in the course of the instruction. This ongoing evaluation by students can affect how much they learn in obvious or subtle ways.

Adults have lived longer than children and therefore bring a multifaceted range of human emotions and personal histories to the learning place. They have learned to mask strong feelings, but these hidden emotions emerge in one way or another, sometimes in puzzling behaviors that may affect learning. A truly wise adult instructor pays attention to these factors and works to foster maximum learning. Even if you are powerless to change attitudes, your awareness of them will boost your effectiveness because you can take steps to override whatever negative attitudes and perceptions your adult students may bring to your classroom. You have important ideas and skills to impart, so why settle for less than the maximum learning from your plans and actions?

The best way to teach adults

I have been teaching adults for more than forty years in a variety of roles, including family life educator, college professor, staff development specialist, pastor, private workshop leader, and trainer of adult instructors. Most recently I spent a year in China teaching English to university students. During these many years, I turned into a participant-observer, studying other students' reactions as well as my own. I logged some important and consistent patterns. These insights and discoveries came from joyful learning successes as well as from some miserable failures. Using this information as my foundation, I decided to create a more formal record of teaching adults.

As I struggled with this task, I finally found a paradigm that brought it all together. I organized the essentials of teaching adults into four instructor styles, and for each style I included five strategies that instructors can employ. During the following years, I taught and tested the model and refined it with the help of many instructors.

I invite you to learn this method and to use it to teach more effectively the topics you love to teach. You may embrace it as *the* way you teach, or you can simply use it to augment other approaches. My goal in writing this book is to affirm and challenge you as you continuously improve the way you teach. Both you and your students will benefit from your willingness to change and grow.

The Teach with Style model

A simple and effective approach

How many teachers are charismatic, engaging, dynamic, and riveting speakers? Most of us are dedicated, ordinary adult instructors who nonetheless have important subjects to teach. The Teach with Style model is a simple, clear, and proven approach to effective adult instruction that makes it unnecessary to be a great speaker. Instead, it outlines some simple guidelines that will help you teach anything well. You will learn techniques for teaching; but more important, you will learn to *manage the dynamics* of the teaching and learning process in order to support growth and change in your adult students.

Two instructor errors

To meet the challenge of teaching adults well, you need to be aware of and avoid making two common instructor errors. First, instructors tend to teach the way they best learn, and second, instructors tend to teach the way they were taught. For example, if you are a visual learner, you will use pictures and diagrams. If you are an auditory learner, you will teach by talking. You may tend to emulate instructors whom you found most effective in teaching, and in doing so, you may not adapt and be flexible when it is necessary. In this book, you will learn to balance four instructor styles to overcome rigid responses and teach as if you were a team of teachers.

Continuous improvement

The Teach with Style model promotes continuous improvement. It helps instructors look closely at their teaching style and seek ways to change and improve. If you use the Teach with Style model it does not mean you have to give up your unique qualities as an instructor. You do not need a complete makeover—you just need to keep improving. The Teach with Style tools help you identify your strengths and build on them. At the same time, you must work on the styles and strategies that you use least in order to develop a balanced approach.

Respond to the diversity of your students

Adult students bring their personal histories with them to class. They express a complex mix of personal, family, and cultural experiences, which influences how they learn and what they know. Instructors must make workshops and classes relevant, appropriate, and anti-biased to respond to such factors as gender, age, ability, language, ethnicity, and spirituality. Our pluralistic society provides us with a great learning opportunity as we exchange outlooks and solutions to problems of life and work. We know more than ever about learning styles and preferences and multiple types of intelligence, so instructors must build learning bridges or risk becoming stale vessels of useless knowledge. *Teach with Style* teaches you to appreciate and respond to this diversity so that all students learn well.

The four instructor styles

The Teach with Style model consists of four instructor styles used to teach adult learners effectively. The four instructor styles are based on four assumptions about how adults learn best. That is, instruction must be *systematic, stimulating, spontaneous,* and *safe* in order to be effective for adult learners. When you apply these four styles in your instructional design, greater learning will result. Each style is equally important and so each must be applied in a balanced way.

Systematic—Adults learn best when they participate in well-planned programs designed cooperatively with other learners. Therefore, the instructor of adults should follow a logically and collaboratively designed plan. This is the Systematic Instructor Style.

The systematic style uses a logical plan that involves the following steps:
- Assess and define needs.
- Set goals and learning objectives.
- Design programs consistent with the objectives.

- Conduct training that matches the plan.
- Evaluate the results of your program.

Adults respond to well-ordered instruction. Learning takes place with less resistance when students are not bogged down trying to figure out what's going on and why things happen the way they do. You should involve the participants in this process whenever possible. If it is not possible to fully engage them in the planning process, you can still solicit their ideas and opinions during the class.

Stimulating—Adults learn best when they are confronted with provocative ideas presented in interesting and lively ways. Therefore, the instructor of adults should use a variety of learning approaches that challenge participants to change. This is the Stimulating Instructor Style.

The stimulating style aims to confront and challenge participants. It might even cause them to feel uncomfortable. Adults need to find new ways to feel, think, and behave. As participants find their old ideas challenged, this process may lead to conflicts between old and new ideas. Learning methods must be active and engaging so that the experience has real impact. The Stimulating Instructor Style helps students discover meaningful solutions for life and work so that they go away excited, prepared, and confident.

Spontaneous—Adults learn best when they experience freedom to explore and try new ideas and behavior. Therefore, the instructor of adults should instill surprise and unpredictability and encourage exploration. This is the Spontaneous Instructor Style.

The spontaneous style is the opposite of the systematic style. Participants need to experience moments with no conscious plan, logic, or reason. The spontaneous experience is valuable for adults because it leads to inventiveness and childlike creativity, and it diminishes judgmental responses. As adults, we seldom experience that kind of liberation in the classroom. The spontaneous experience includes humor, fun, creative expression, storytelling, risk taking, and meditative reflection. These impromptu moments can inspire wisdom beyond the confines of an agenda or conventional thought. At first glance this may seem frivolous, but these events can become turning points in understanding and personal growth.

When balanced with a logical plan, allowing time for participants to explore and discover creates a nice milieu for creativity and learning. We know where we are headed, so side trips are feasible to follow current interests without getting too far afield. Allowing a group to dream up the answers to questions is sometimes better than looking for calculated responses. Laughter is refreshing and cleansing and often leads to innovation. We need to see problems in a new light in order to make changes. Many instructors want to keep tight control of the schedule, so allowing these moments may not be easy. Freedom to explore often serves the participants well, however.

Safe—Adults learn best when they are in a safe, trust-filled learning environment. Therefore, the instructor of adults should create a safe learning place for participants. This is the Safe Instructor Style.

The Safe Instructor Style is the opposite of the stimulating style. A safe environment includes adequate arrangements for creature comforts, such as rest rooms, appetizing drinks and snacks, adequate breaks, and a comfortable room arrangement.

Participants feel safe when they know they will not be ridiculed, pressured, or manipulated, and when they play a part in how the learning experience proceeds. Participants feel safe when they are allowed the freedom to interact with others without undue force or embarrassment.

Safety means that a participant's ideas may be challenged, but there is respect for individual differences and points of view. Make it clear to adult participants that they may choose not to participate in any part of the program if it poses undue risk or discomfort, and then provide alternate, substitute activities, or encourage participants to suggest a compromise plan. The basic goal of the Safe Instructor Style is to help people make a transition into learning and to remain open and relaxed in the learning environment. This begins even before students arrive, and it should continue throughout the experience.

The lists of characteristics of the four instructor styles (Table 1-1) will help you grasp the basic idea of each instructor style. Each style can meet the needs of adult learners and enable them to learn in the way that is best for them. In chapters to follow, you will learn what strategies to use for each style.

TABLE 1-1

Characteristics of Instructor Styles

Systematic Instructor Style
Follow a logically and collaboratively designed plan.

Logical
Clear agenda
Stated objective
Behavioral outcome
Orderly
Clear
Sensible
Planned
Purposeful
Obtainable goals
Sequential
No loose ends
Predictable

Spontaneous Instructor Style
Encourage exploration, surprise, and unpredictability.

Unpredictable
Exploration
Free expression
Imagination
Creative
Artistry
Poetry
Music
Drama
Surprise
Humor
Risk taking
Wildness

Stimulating Instructor Style
Use active learning approaches and challenge participants to change.

Challenging
Provocative
Dynamic
Active
Exciting
Energetic
Motivating
Innovative
Creative tension
Progressive
Inspirational
Electric
Lively

Safe Instructor Style
Create a safe learning place for participants.

Comfortable
Peaceful
Pleasant
Accepting
Relaxed
Calm
Trusting
Open
Restful
Mellow
Protective
Harmonious
Responsive

The best instruction balances these four instructor styles. This is demonstrated in chapter 6 with a sample workshop called "What's My Style?" At this point, it is only necessary to realize how important it is to balance the four styles, which will result in the best adult teaching. The following table shows how the four styles can be used together in teaching adult learners (Table 1-2).

TABLE 1-2

Balance the Four Instructor Styles

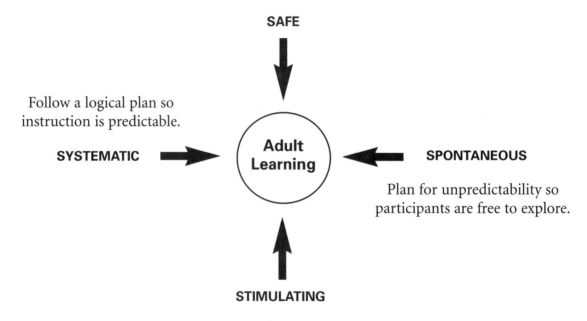

Help participants feel at ease, comfortable, and welcome.

Follow a logical plan so instruction is predictable.

Plan for unpredictability so participants are free to explore.

Provoke, motivate, and challenge participants to change.

TABLE 1-3

Overview: Instructor Styles and Strategies

Use this style:	Because:	Use these strategies:
SYSTEMATIC Set shared goals, plan for agreed-upon results, and measure success.	Adults are more likely to change when they participate in well-planned programs designed cooperatively.	1. Collaborate with participants as you plan. 2. Assess participant learning needs and styles. 3. Set clear, meaningful goals. 4. Plan to reach your goals. 5. Evaluate your plan.
STIMULATING Actively challenge adults to think, change, and grow.	Adults will be able to make positive changes when they encounter ideas presented in interesting and lively ways.	6. Present information in interesting, useful ways 7. Use active learning approaches. 8. Encourage creativity. 9. Help participants solve real problems. 10. Help participants practice new learning.
SPONTANEOUS Plan and allow for play, humor, and surprise in the learning experience.	Adults need the opportunity and permission to try out new ways of seeing and behaving to break free from old patterns.	11. Help participants tell their stories. 12. Make it funny, make it fun. 13. Use imagination and the arts. 14. Build in risk taking. 15. Take time to reflect.
SAFE Create comfort zones for adults to take risks in learning.	Adults need an accepting, trust-filled environment in order to let go of the old and embrace the new.	16. Help participants feel at home. 17. Let participants know what to expect. 18. Help participants get acquainted. 19. Keep time commitments. 20. Build trust and openness.

Instructor strategies and learning activities

The four instructor *styles* are the fundamental, non-negotiable conditions needed to ensure your success as a teacher of adults. Instructor strategies are the main ingredients of each instructor style. You might imagine the instructor strategies as the building blocks for each instructor style. A strategy guides the selection of the specific learning *activities* you use to teach.

The Overview: Instructor Styles and Strategies (Table 1-3) provides a quick look at the instructor styles and strategies as well as a quick reference to plan training.

The more you use strategies from each of the instructor style categories, the better. You will find that you tend to use some strategies more often than you do others. The strategies you seldom use will be the ones you need to practice and improve. You probably have a natural talent to use some strategies, so work on the ones that take you out of your comfort zone. Inexperienced instructors may need to do much work. More seasoned instructors may need to break longtime habits or simply "tune up" certain strategies.

Your instruction takes shape through the learning activities you use. Participants experience the activities, but they are not necessarily aware of the styles and strategies that guide your actions. The particular cluster of strategies used to influence participants demonstrates an instructor's style. The most effective instructors use a broad range of strategies. They must be sensitive observers who are able to adjust their instruction to the unique and diverse needs of adult learners. This kind of instruction results in adult participants who are motivated and open to change and therefore better prepared for life and work.

The strategies with related learning activities are covered in detail in chapters 2, 3, 4, and 5. A sample instructor strategy and a learning activity for each instructor style are presented in the following table (Table 1-4).

TABLE 1-4

Sample Instructor Strategies and Learning Activities

INSTRUCTOR STYLES	SAMPLE STRATEGY	SAMPLE LEARNING ACTIVITY
Systematic Instructor Style	Assess participant learning needs and styles.	Interview participants as they enter the classroom to determine why they came to the workshop. Use a flip chart or overhead projector to record each answer.
Stimulating Instructor Style	Help participants solve real problems.	Have the participants contribute their actual job problems in class so your instruction is centered on these important job-related concerns.
Spontaneous Instructor Style	Build in risk taking.	Assign participants to small work groups and have each group take responsibility for teaching a portion of the class.
Safe Instructor Style	Help participants feel at home.	Arrange seating in a circle before the class starts and greet participants warmly as they arrive.

The organization of *Teach with Style*

This book is divided into eight chapters. The four styles with their respective strategies and learning activities are presented in chapters 2 through 5:

- Chapter 2: The Systematic Instructor Style
- Chapter 3: The Stimulating Instructor Style
- Chapter 4: The Spontaneous Instructor Style
- Chapter 5: The Safe Instructor Style

In these chapters, you will learn the twenty instructor *strategies* and more than 150 ideas and learning activities to help you teach effectively. In chapter 6, Planning for Balanced Instruction, you will learn how to balance the four styles by studying a sample workshop for child care managers. Chapter 7,

Practical Application of the Instructor Styles, Strategies, and Learning Activities: A Workshop, shows how to implement the model by tracing the process of an actual workshop for child care providers from planning through implementation. It shows how the specific learning activities can be selected to provide an interesting and useful program for participants. Chapter 8, Plan Your Continuous Improvement, presents tools and inventories for planning your continuous improvement as an instructor of adults.

Summary

The four instructor styles—systematic, stimulating, spontaneous, and safe—address the four ways in which adults learn best. You can effectively teach adult learners by applying these four styles in a balanced way in your instructional design. Now that you have a sense of the whole, let's turn to a discussion of each individual style.

The Systematic Instructor Style: Strategies and learning activities

Adults learn more when they participate in well-planned programs that are designed cooperatively. Systematic instruction is characterized by shared goals, a program that reaches the goals, and evaluation of progress toward the goals. The systematic strategies and learning activities in this chapter will help you design instruction so that it flows logically from learning needs to learning outcomes.

Systematic strategies include the following:

- Strategy 1—Collaborate with participants as you plan
- Strategy 2—Assess participant learning needs and styles
- Strategy 3—Set clear, meaningful goals
- Strategy 4—Plan to reach your goals
- Strategy 5—Evaluate your plan

Systematic Strategy 1—Collaborate with participants as you plan

Collaborative instruction should be well targeted and flexible in meeting participant needs. When possible, consult directly with the participants as you plan. Involve participants before and during the course of instruction to make the experience relevant to their needs. Be willing to shift the program, when warranted, and openly share the consequences of doing so with your participants.

Participants are more likely to learn when they take ownership of the learning experience. Meet directly with a group of participants early on to involve them in planning. Teaching is a partnership between participant and teacher. Ideally, you will get to know the participants before and during the course of instruction so you can plan together for the best instructional fit.

Do not be afraid to relinquish some of your control (or to hang on where needed). Just be clear about which aspects of the instructional experience are negotiable and which are not. In some circumstances very little is negotiable (for example, in a highly structured academic setting), and in others the sky is the limit (for example, in an informal community class). Make sure you are not holding onto control just for your own comfort. Listen to your participants and modify your instruction to meet their needs.

The following activities will help you plan a workshop or course collaboratively with participants.

Activity 1.1: A learning team approach

PURPOSE: To facilitate self-directed group learning.

DESCRIPTION: Instruct the participants to select members for these roles: The Leader acts as facilitator for the planning, the Recorder acts as the team's memory, and the Observer stays in the background and provides information on how the group is working. The instructor also stays in the background and makes himself available to consult and guide when needed. The participant facilitator leads this six-step process:

1. Discuss, list, and record the needs and interests of the group.
2. From this list, choose those that are most vital to the group, and more clearly define and prioritize them.
3. Use this list to make a learning schedule of topics and set learning goals for each.
4. Discuss, list, and record all the resources and learning techniques for reaching each goal. Assign a topic to each member or team.
5. Each member or team takes a topic to research and present to the group.
6. The instructor acts as consultant to each teacher or teaching team.

Activity 1.2: Representative group

PURPOSE: To collaborate with a small group of representatives.

DESCRIPTION: People are selected to act as representatives because they are able to reflect the group's thoughts about learning needs. The instructor meets with the representatives one or more times to assess learning needs. Prepare open-ended questions, and be ready to follow the lead of the representatives. When you feel you have a good grasp of what is needed, present this to the representatives for their comments. When they agree with your assessment, you can ask them to return to the larger group they represent to see if the larger group agrees as well, and if so, proceed with planning the curriculum.

Activity 1.3: On-the-spot collaboration

PURPOSE: To collaborate when time is short or when there has been no opportunity to gather information or meet with participants or their representatives.

DESCRIPTION: If you are not able to collaborate prior to the session, you should at least spend some time determining the participants' needs and expectations at the beginning of the class so you can modify your plans to better meet participant needs. Tell participants what is planned and what the parameters are for adjusting the method and content of the instruction. Solicit opinions and ideas from the group and let them know what is and is not realistic. Take whatever time you have available for this. It will be time well spent.

Activity 1.4: Interviews with managers

PURPOSE: To plan a session's content and collaborate with leaders so that learning will be validated and will support later on-the-job application of learning.

DESCRIPTION: Make the effort to talk with decision makers when you plan instruction. Get their input to add to the mix. In fact, they may be the power brokers that make or break the learning experience. Sometimes you become the liaison between participant and employer.

For example, a continuing education director of a community college asked a trainer to train her instructors on how to teach better. The trainer had no opportunity to meet with this group of people before the session to find out what their needs were. The director had some definite ideas she wanted him to get across. They were able to agree that the trainer would dedicate a small section of the workshop to the director's points and balance them with the needs of the group of instructors as they expressed them in the training.

Activity 1.5: On-the-spot interviews

PURPOSE: To quickly assess participants' needs and interests and collaborate with them in planning.

DESCRIPTION: The instructor can quickly assess learning directly from participants as they arrive. This is particularly effective in conference workshops where the instructor has little time to collaborate with participants on content or methods. Prepare questions in advance and meet individually with participants as they arrive to get their input. Make a list of your findings and present this to the rest of the class when they are assembled.

If your class extends over several sessions, you can plan to question participants several times to see if they are getting what they need and if they understand your instruction. Make periodic reports to the class and modify your instruction according to the feedback you receive.

Activity 1.6: Small-group in-session collaboration

PURPOSE: To collaborate after a session has begun.

DESCRIPTION: Sometimes you may feel you have not targeted your instruction as well as you could have. It's not too late to collaborate and make adjustments. Take a break from learning and explain to the participants that you need more input from them to help you teach more effectively. Divide the class into small groups and have each group look over the syllabus (objectives and agenda) and provide feedback to you about it. Some formats for small-group work include the following:

- Take ten minutes in your groups to design the ideal workshop on your topic, _____.
- In your small groups, decide what topics are most important to you. Then describe how you would like to learn about them. Be ready to report in fifteen minutes.
- Look over the syllabus (objectives and agenda for the workshop) on your own and make notes. Then meet with your small group and suggest improvements. Be prepared to explain and discuss your suggestions.

Activity 1.7: The collaborative attitude

PURPOSE: The collaborative attitude makes collaboration a normal part of your teaching.

DESCRIPTION: This is not so much an activity as an approach to teaching and learning. Listen carefully to the feelings, perceptions, and opinions of your participants. Look at their faces and body posture as you teach. What do you see? If you find that things are dragging, people are taking long breaks, or lots of side talking is happening, it may be time to check in with your participants. Do not be afraid to stop the process and use one of the methods above to readjust. Reluctant participants will learn very little.

Systematic Strategy 2—Assess participant learning needs and styles

Instruction should be based on participant needs, interests, and learning styles. Diversity issues must be considered. Pay attention to the accessibility of facilities, special learning needs, and anti-bias concerns. Determine how participants best receive, integrate, and express information.

It is rare in formal education, from first grade to graduate school, to find serious attempts made to find out what the participants want to learn. This is usually considered the purpose of the term paper or special project. Traditionally, participants are spooned the academic medicine prescribed by the system. Wise and prudent adult educators avoid carrying on that tradition. Get acquainted with your participants. Discover their learning needs and desires and be responsive to them. Consider combining different assessment methods for more accurate results.

The following activities will help you assess participants' needs and learning styles.

Activity 2.1: The inventory

PURPOSE: To gather information that can be easily and quickly analyzed.

DESCRIPTION: An inventory is a written assessment received directly from the participants or organizational personnel. Questionnaires, checklists, or surveys are common forms of inventories. These inventories ask questions about needs and interests of participants, and then the data is analyzed in preparation for instruction. Instruction is designed around prevalent needs, interests, or learning styles.

ADVANTAGES: Inventories are usually easy to administer, inexpensive, and confidential, and they take little time.

DISADVANTAGES: Sometimes inventories get a low return rate, give sketchy results, or are hard to interpret.

Instructors can use the inventories in Tables 2-1 and 2-2 to assess the learning styles of participants in classes or workshops. Instructors can distribute them to participants before a workshop, tally information, and adjust teaching strategies accordingly. Participants can also fill them out at the beginning of a workshop. A tally can be made during a break and then adjustments can be made for the rest of the learning experience. The instructors themselves can take the inventories to gain some information about their own learning styles.

How Do You Learn Best? (Table 2-1) is a learning style inventory that examines how participants best receive, integrate, and demonstrate knowledge and skills. The Learner Styles Inventory (Table 2-2) may also be helpful in determining the learning styles of your participants based on the Teach with Style model.

TABLE 2-1

How Do You Learn Best?

Instructions: The learning cycle includes (1) receiving, (2) exploring and integrating, and (3) demonstrating competence in knowledge, skill, or understanding in a particular subject area. Check three to five methods in each category that suit you best while learning.

How do you best RECEIVE knowledge, skill, or understanding?

❑ Stories, anecdotes, illustrations
❑ Charts, graphs
❑ Lectures
❑ Short talks, "lecturettes"
❑ Question-and-answer sessions
❑ Reading
❑ Films, videos
❑ Logical sequencing
❑ Bits and pieces
❑ Surprise and humor
❑ Lots of repetition
❑ Demonstrations

❑ Case studies
❑ Simulations and games
❑ Personal coaching/mentoring
❑ Peer learning
❑ Computer programs
❑ Home study
❑ Classroom
❑ Self-directed learning
❑ Overhead, flip charts
❑ _____
❑ _____
❑ _____

How do you like to EXPLORE AND INTEGRATE knowledge, skill, or understanding?

❑ Small-group discussion
❑ Large-group discussion
❑ Write a report
❑ Do a research project
❑ Small-group assignments
❑ Problem solving, puzzles, and challenges
❑ Art work, drawing, sculpting, etc.
❑ Dialogue with one other person
❑ Simulations and games

❑ Demonstrations
❑ Debates
❑ Role-play
❑ Guided imagery
❑ Journaling
❑ Meditating, pondering
❑ _____
❑ _____
❑ _____

How do you like to DEMONSTRATE your new learning?

❑ Take a written test
❑ Essay test
❑ True/false, multiple choice
❑ Photo essay
❑ Live demonstration
❑ Group project
❑ Make a statistical chart
❑ Keep a journal
❑ Give a talk
❑ Set up an experiment

❑ Teach it to someone else
❑ Engage in a debate or discussion
❑ Produce a video
❑ Dramatic presentation or skit
❑ Present a small-group report
❑ Do a mind map
❑ Role-play
❑ _____
❑ _____
❑ _____

My Learning Style
Reflect on your responses and write a brief summary of how you like to learn.

TABLE 2-2

Learner Styles Inventory

Instructions: Check the boxes that most represent your favorite ways to learn. Add the number of checks to get learning style scores.

LEARNER STYLE	LEARNING ACTIVITY	LEARNER STYLE	LEARNING ACTIVITY
SYSTEMATIC	❑ Case studies ❑ Charts and graphs ❑ Clear goals and objectives ❑ Well-organized lectures ❑ Computer programs ❑ Well-outlined topics ❑ Expert panel discussion ❑ Written material or handouts ❑ Structured classroom seating ❑ Taking lecture notes ❑ Using workbooks ❑ Written, objective tests Systematic Style Score: _____	**SPONTANEOUS**	❑ Drawing, sculpting, and so on ❑ Drama or role-playing ❑ Creating and inventing ❑ Guided imagination ❑ Journaling ❑ Fun activities and games ❑ Meditating ❑ Mind mapping ❑ Storytelling ❑ Surprise and humor ❑ Taking risks ❑ Poetry and music Spontaneous Style Score: _____
STIMULATING	❑ Active learning approaches ❑ Debates ❑ Demonstrations ❑ Dynamic, short presentations ❑ Clear principles ❑ Group projects ❑ Examples and illustrations ❑ Time to practice ❑ Question-and-answer period ❑ Solving real-life problems ❑ Teach others ❑ Guided group discussions Stimulating Style Score: _____	**SAFE**	❑ Friendly instructor ❑ Get acquainted/warm-up exercises ❑ Good refreshments ❑ Group projects ❑ Know what will happen ❑ Mentoring ❑ Nice learning space ❑ Peer learning ❑ Personal coaching ❑ Relaxed atmosphere ❑ Self-study programs ❑ Small-group discussion Safe Style Score: _____

List some other ways you like to learn:

What advice would you give the instructor(s) to make the learning most effective and enjoyable for you?

Activity 2.2: The interview

PURPOSE: To acquire in-depth opinions of participant needs.

DESCRIPTION: Interviews can be done individually or in a group. They can be used as a follow-up to other needs assessments or as a stand-alone method. The interviewer(s) may ask some of the same questions as in an inventory, and then ask questions to clarify.

ADVANTAGES: A precise diagnosis of participant needs is possible, and a face-to-face analysis allows assessment of feelings and opinions as well as facts. It provides a human touch.

DISADVANTAGES: It is time consuming and may not provide a broad picture. Anonymity is not possible.

Activity 2.3: Inquiry

PURPOSE: This activity provides a systematic analysis of information or data that is already available.

DESCRIPTION: Analyze complaints from the community or parents, statistics on staff turnover or accidents, child care staff comments, supervisor evaluations, and so on. Much information can be found that will give clues to learning needs. You can follow up your analysis of this data with inventories or interviews. Make sure confidentiality is maintained and proper authorizations are secured.

ADVANTAGES: It is convenient, does not take up workers' time, and uses objective rather than subjective information.

DISADVANTAGES: When taken alone, inquiries do not identify causes. Information may be misinterpreted because it is only as good as the data available.

Activity 2.4: Direct observation

PURPOSE: Direct observation provides concrete examples of learning knowledge and ability.

DESCRIPTION: Observation requires great skill and a clear purpose on the part of an observer or facilitator. The observer uses clear-cut criteria to observe participants while they demonstrate knowledge and skill either in simulation or in real-life conditions. The observer determines what instruction is needed based on the analysis.

ADVANTAGE: Observation provides a clear diagnosis of participant needs.

DISADVANTAGES: Observation requires a skilled assessment facilitator; it is time consuming; and the mere fact of being observed may influence the behavior of the person being observed.

Use the Observer Inventory in chapter 8 to assess instructors based on the Teach with Style model.

Activity 2.5: Examination

PURPOSE: To determine learning needs by testing participants.

DESCRIPTION: The examiner administers written, oral, or experiential tests to participants to determine their level of knowledge, skill, or understanding. The best tests are those that have been certified by research and proven to accurately assess participants. Many such tests are available in many fields of learning.

ADVANTAGE: Provides an objective measure of needs or learning styles.

DISADVANTAGES: May not be useful with those who do not take tests very well and may be expensive to administer.

Activity 2.6: Informal discussions

PURPOSE: To provide an informal way for participants to communicate their needs and interests to the instructor.

DESCRIPTION: Informal discussion with a whole class or small groups before and during instruction can be helpful for getting a picture of participant needs, interests, and learning styles. The "I wish . . ." exercise found in Safe Strategy 18 is an example of this. The idea is to pose an assessment question for discussion, then let the group respond to it and report responses to the instructor or to the entire group of participants. The instructor adjusts the instruction based on this information.

Activity 2.7: Listing and voting

PURPOSE: Listing and voting allows members of a class or workshop to help determine content and methods.

DESCRIPTION: The instructor may bring a defined curriculum and set methods, but flexibility in this helps learning. Listing and voting gives participants a chance to take a part in determining the learning content, which builds ownership. The instructor can provide the basic information or solicit it from the participants. Begin by listing all the options (topics for study, methods of learning, and so on). Then let participants vote on the options they think will be most important to them. One way to vote is to have participants place colored dots (each color having a value) next to their favorite item on a flip chart. In this way, participants "spend" their dots as they choose. Participants may also first lobby for their own choices to convince others and then cast their votes. The instructor uses the results of the voting to determine or adjust course content and methods.

Systematic Strategy 3—Set clear, meaningful goals

Carefully formulated and articulated goals and objectives should be based on the instructor's assessment of the needs and interests of participants. Make these goals and objectives available for review. An instructor should be able to say specifically what participants can be expected to gain by taking the class or workshop session. Sometimes specific behavioral or performance objectives are best; for example, "After viewing a video on child safety, you will be able to identify at least five safety problems in a photograph of a toddler-age classroom." Sometimes a more general goal is appropriate, such as "You will feel more relaxed." Whether goals are specific or general, make sure that participants know how they will benefit from the instruction.

Clear goals help adult participants know whether your instruction will meet their needs and expectations. Clear goals make it possible to know if your instruction is on target throughout the workshop or learning experience. How often have you sat in a workshop wondering where things were headed? Adults will often allow a class to drift rather than risk challenging the teacher. It is fair and prudent to have clear learning goals to guide your instruction.

Goals and objectives are like a list of benefits you gain by buying a product or service. As you plan, think how your participants will gain from participation in your workshop or course. Think of your participants as customers. Teaching is rarely thought of as a matter of an exchange of participants' time, energy, or money for knowledge. However, participants (and their organizations) should clearly benefit from their investment.

The following activities will help you to set clear, meaningful goals in your teaching.

Activity 3.1: Reversing the problem or need

PURPOSE: This activity presents an easy and useful way to create objectives or goals.

DESCRIPTION: Although making clear goal statements is not always easy, one way to do it is to turn a problem or need into a positive statement. If you don't know what types of play activities preschool children like, but you face a group of them daily, then your goal would be "to know what activities preschool children like"—that's all there is to it! Just reverse the need or problem by stating its opposite. If you can state your problem, you can state your goal.

Use the Goal Statement Practice examples in Table 2-3 to practice writing a goal statement from the problem statement. (Cover up the last column as you practice, and then check your work.)

TABLE 2-3

Goal Statement Practice

Problem	Fill in your goal statement	Examples
My students need to know all the standard steps in diapering an infant.	_____ _____ _____ _____	1. The students will be able to list the standard steps in diapering an infant. 2. You will be able to diaper an infant using all necessary steps.
Our employees have not learned to use the new network e-mail.	_____ _____ _____ _____	1. All the employees will be able to e-mail using the new system. 2. You will be able to use the new network e-mail.
The child care managers have goals but don't know how to develop action steps to reach them.	_____ _____ _____ _____	1. The child care managers will be able to define action steps for each organizational goal. 2. The child care managers will know how to reach goals by listing related action steps.

Activity 3.2: Three levels of learning—understanding, knowledge, and skill

PURPOSE: This activity presents three ways to state goals to meet all instructional content.

DESCRIPTION: These three content goals—understanding, knowledge, and skill—are simple to use and cover the range of what you will teach. Use the chart below (Table 2-4) as a guide to determine what content goals you will use. Remember that one content goal may overlap another, so use the chart flexibly and creatively to write clear goals.

TABLE 2-4

Content Goals Guide

Content Goal	Discussion	Examples
UNDERSTAND—the ability to interpret the meaning of events, define causes, and comprehend values and truth	This is the broadest and deepest content you can teach. A goal to understand directs one to teach wisdom and generate a global view of things. It is also about why things happen and if they should happen. Understanding is needed by leaders and politicians as well as by those who change diapers and play circle games with preschoolers.	1. The student will explain how interactions with the care provider are vital to the child's development. 2. Write a description of a child care manager who has the courage and insight to motivate her or his employees to excellence. 3. Given three behavioral management scenarios, the participant will explain how and why the child care provider could have been more effective in teaching children good behavior.
KNOW—the ability to recall facts and principles and apply them in solving problems	The knowing of something goes beyond just reciting facts to being able to use the knowledge to solve problems or make progress toward solutions. Seeing the principles involved enables a person to move beyond rote or habit to making judgments about the facts. Knowing involves being able to juxtapose, compare, and discriminate in order to make decisions.	1. Identify six reasons to involve parents in school-age after-school programs. 2. Be able to list the ways to stop bleeding, and tell the proper use of the tourniquet. 3. Write a brief history of child care in the state, and name some key people in its development. 4. Name five "best practice" principles covered in the workshop handouts.

(continues on p. 24)

Content Goals Guide, continued

Content Goal	Discussion	Examples
GAIN SKILL—the ability to do something well, to perform tasks with efficiency and effectiveness resulting in a process or product that meets certain standards	A skill is something you do at a certain level of proficiency. Skills may be either common or unique, but the person who has the ability does it so that a standard is met with the least effort and the greatest achievement of a goal.	1. Be able to demonstrate the proper use of a fire extinguisher. 2. Be able to delegate appropriate tasks and follow up with supportive coaching. 3. Wash your hands so that no dirt residue remains.

Activity 3.3: Process goals

PURPOSE: To guide your instructional design.

DESCRIPTION: In addition to *content* goals that include understanding, knowledge, and skill, you can use *process* goals to meet the instructional method standards you want to reach. Do you want to spend at least 25 percent of the time at the beginning of a workshop for warm-up and getting acquainted? This is a process goal. Do you want to get lots of participation in the session? Do you want to develop a mentoring system in your child care classes? These are process goals. Process goals are usually not published; they are your personal guidelines that describe how you instruct. When you work toward greater balance in using all the instructor styles and strategies, you will want to have process goals to help you plan improvement in your instruction.

Activity 3.4: Personal goals

PURPOSE: Personal goals help participants individualize learning outcomes.

DESCRIPTION: Improve the effectiveness of your instruction by allowing participants to identify their own personal learning goals. This can be done at the beginning, middle, or end of a workshop, conference, or class. Ask participants to write a personalized goal they want to reach as a result of the learning event. For example, a child care worker taking a class in curriculum design might write, "I want to go beyond just entertaining my kids and add more real learning to my activities." Have participants write goals at the beginning to help them focus and take advantage of the experiences ahead, or do this later on to allow participants an opportunity to become familiar with the subject matter so that more precise personal goals can be set. At the end of the event, you can send participants away with personal goals to achieve as they apply the learning.

Some ways to help participants set personal goals include the following:

- Give all participants a card and ask them to write goals on one side and how they might reach the goals on the other.
- Establish partners (or small groups) to work as a team to help each other set personal goals. The partners or team members can help each other throughout the workshop or in the future to keep the commitments made to reach these goals.
- At the end of a learning event, have participants write goals on a card with their e-mail addresses or telephone numbers listed (if they are comfortable doing this). These can be handed to another person for follow-up or distributed randomly with instructions to contact the person in three months to check on progress. They can also be slipped into self-addressed envelopes and sent to participants by the instructor.
- Ask participants to write "self-contracts" by recording goals they wish to achieve.

Activity 3.5: Getting agreement on goals

PURPOSE: This activity forms a partnership for learning.

DESCRIPTION: The process of getting agreement on goals between instructor and participants may be a formal or a very informal arrangement. Sometimes the simple process of signing up for a course or a conference can be considered "agreement." In a one-hour class on how to be a better listener, there is an assumption that the instructor will teach an introduction only on that topic. If, on the other hand, the instructor only covers introductory material in an all-day workshop, you will feel cheated. Publish specific objectives so participants will know what to expect.

The following methods can be used to reach agreement with participants:

- State objectives and allow participants to vote on or rank the ones they want most.
- Ask the participants to review the class objectives; allow participants to raise questions or objections in group discussion. Read each objective and have them simply nod their heads if they agree.
- State the objectives, content, and methods of the class. Call for a break and let those who want to leave exit the room. Those who remain have agreed with the stated goals.
- Allow participants to discuss the course syllabus or outline and suggest changes. If none are suggested, you have an agreement. If changes are proposed, renegotiate.
- Make a more formal agreement by writing out the goals and responsibilities of participants and instructor and have each of the parties sign it.

Activity 3.6: Publish the goals

PURPOSE: This activity encourages instructors to be clear and open about goals.

DESCRIPTION: Writing goals is important. All involved are able to track progress toward them if they are published. Here are some ways to publish goals:

- General goals should be published at the first announcement of a learning event so participants can choose knowledgeably.
- Publish instructional goals on a handout or on the first page of participant materials.
- Write them on a flip chart, overhead, or whiteboard. This allows you to make changes.
- Draw a box next to each objective so you can check off each objective as it is met.
- Go back over the objectives when you complete the instruction as a means of review for you and the participants.

Activity 3.7: A standard goal—enjoy learning

PURPOSE: This standard goal reminds instructors to make learning enjoyable.

DESCRIPTION: Always put "enjoy learning" at the end of your list of goals.

Participants will be pleased and relieved that you are going to make this experience enjoyable for them. It is a reminder that, although teaching and learning are hard work, you can still have fun in the process.

Systematic Strategy 4—Plan to reach your goals

This strategy supports instruction that is based on, and achieves, the objectives. If necessary, be willing to renegotiate with participants to adjust the program or goals. When the program is completed, the participants should report in the evaluation whether they learned what they needed and wanted to learn. For example, if you tell participants that they are going to learn how to promote development of gross-motor skills in infants, that is what they should be able to do by the end of the learning experience. What happens in the instruction should match precisely the objectives, goals, or purpose.

Your instructional program should flow naturally from your goals, just as goals flow naturally from the assessment of needs. The message of this book is to plan instruction that balances the four styles. Once you are ready to design your instruction, remember to balance the four styles to make it systematic, stimulating, spontaneous, and safe. Make sure you are able to use all the strategies that support those styles.

The following activities will help you plan to meet your instructional goals.

Activity 4.1: Have an agenda

PURPOSE: To provide a visual means for keeping on track.

DESCRIPTION: An agenda, syllabus, or outline that you and your participants follow keeps things on target. This can be as simple as a list of topics and activities on a flip chart or as formal as a printed agenda. The important thing is to publish your path toward your goals. Follow it just as you would a map that outlines the route to your destination.

Here is a sample agenda for a two-hour class titled "Be a Better Listener":

Objectives:

Know the importance of listening.

Experience the benefits of listening.

Improve your listening skills.

Agenda:

7:00 p.m.   Introduction and the importance of listening (lecturette)

7:15 p.m.   Warm-up and getting acquainted (small-group activity)

7:30 p.m.   How to listen (handout)

7:45 p.m.   How to—and how not to—listen (demonstration)

8:00 p.m.   Listening practice with feedback (small-group exercise)

8:45 p.m.   Wrap-up and evaluation

Activity 4.2: Organize instruction

PURPOSE: This helps participants take logical steps toward the goals.

DESCRIPTION: Here are some ways to organize instruction:

- Simple to complex. Begin with the simplest aspects of a topic and move toward more complex learning. For example, a child moves from mounting and balancing a bicycle to steering and braking.

- Logical progression. In teaching an introduction to child care, you might begin by teaching the history and background of the field, then move on to cover the current philosophies and practices. Next, you may turn to some more practical aspects such as working with groups of children, one's suitability for this field, or a field visit to a child care center.

- Beginning, middle, and end. Teaching a class is just like writing an article or book. You begin at the beginning with some kind of introduction, move into the body of the text, and then come to a conclusion.

For some other ways of organizing instruction, see Activity 6.2: Sequencing.

Activity 4.3: Renegotiate as needed

PURPOSE: Renegotiating keeps instruction on track.

DESCRIPTION: Periodically check to see if you are on target. If you find you are not reaching your goals, you may need to renegotiate them. The problem may stem from having made an incorrect assessment of participants' needs; in this case you need to reassess. Or the source of the problem may be incorrect goal statements; you need to restate the goals. The problem may be in using the wrong methods; you will need to change your methods. Do not be hesitant to readjust and renegotiate—you want to reach the right goals in behalf of your participants.

Activity 4.4: Actively encourage learning

PURPOSE: Instructors should actively encourage learning to reach goals.

DESCRIPTION: Use every moment to create conditions that encourage participants to take responsibility for their own learning. Strive to facilitate curiosity, a search for truth, and continuous improvement. Here are some suggestions to accomplish this:

- Ask questions. Ask more questions; give fewer answers.
- Form study/work groups. Encourage cooperative learning.
- Be slow to speak. Do not be so quick to make your points; draw out the points from your participants.
- Point the way. Do not lead the participants, but get them going in the right direction.
- Model curiosity and truth seeking. Be a searcher yourself as a model for your participants. Let them in on your quest for answers.
- Open dialogue. Promote mutual discovery and less structured teaching.

Activity 4.5: Instructor planning notes

PURPOSE: Planning notes balance your instructional planning.

DESCRIPTION: Use the Instructor Planning Notes form (see chapter 6, Table 6-1) to plan instruction that balances the four instructor styles. This form guides you through a planning sequence. It begins with the systematic style to set the proper direction for your instruction. Next, you are asked to create learning that is stimulating and challenging. Then you try to find ways to make learning spontaneous and fun, and finally, create plans for helping participants feel comfortable.

TABLE 2-5

Sample Instructional Module

Title of the Module _____
Give it a title that is clever or humorous.

Learning objectives: *List what students will take away from this event—how will they change?*

_____

_____

_____

Procedures (steps to take): *Spell out the exact steps for your lesson and the timing for each step. You may want to put this in actual time during the session.*

_____

_____

_____

Materials needed: *Here list everything you'll need to be ready for the module.*

_____

_____

_____

Options to modify procedures: *List any changes that could be made depending on the situation. You may or may not need them.*

_____

_____

_____

Evaluation design: *Be ready with a way to measure your success—there should be a way to measure whether you met each objective listed.*

_____

_____

_____

TABLE 2-6

Sample Matrix

Module Title	Objectives	Methods	Materials	Options/Time	Evaluation
Introduction and warm-up	Prepare to learn	Pairs of participants interview each other and take notes. Test accuracy.	Interview handout with spaces to take notes	10 minutes—5 minutes each. Expand this if it is working well.	Did you feel prepared to listen?
The importance of listening	Motivate to learn	Lecturette using the 10 reasons to listen.	Handout/overhead projector and transparencies	15 minutes with Q&A. Option: Have participants work in pairs to learn these and then ask them for a reaction.	Do you want to listen better now?
When did you really feel listened to in your life?	Feel the value of listening	Groups of four—They share when you feel listened to and how it felt. Groups share with whole class.	Flip chart/pens/tape	30 minutes. Let groups write their own lists on flip chart paper.	Do you value listening more now as a result of this class?

. . . and so forth

31

Activity 4.6: Instructional module guide

PURPOSE: This guide provides a template when planning instruction.

DESCRIPTION: Planning can be made easier by dividing your class or workshop into a series of related but separate modules. There are many ways to design these. An instructional module guide is a standardized outline you can use when designing lessons. You can use the example in Table 2-5, or put together your own form to help you plan the modules in a class or workshop.

Activity 4.7: Design matrix

PURPOSE: This design matrix aids in planning instruction.

DESCRIPTION: A matrix is a simple visual presentation of your instructional plan. One way to use a matrix is to list the essential elements across the top to form columns (objectives, methods, materials, and so on). Along the side, list the sequence for each part of your presentation. An example of a matrix is presented on the previous page in Table 2-6. You can add or modify this design to fit your own particular planning needs. (Another example of a matrix can be found in chapter 7, Table 7-1, Workshop Agenda.)

Systematic Strategy 5—Evaluate your plan

This strategy helps you assess the degree to which the teaching experience meets the objectives, makes this information available to the participants, and offers suggestions if future training is needed.

Remember that planning is a process that encourages instructors to involve participants, assess learning needs, set goals, and plan to reach them. The last step is to check whether your plan and your instructional methods worked. Did you reach your goals? Did participants gain the understanding, knowledge, and skills they needed? There are many ways to check your results.

Whether simple or complex, evaluating results is a necessary step to increase effectiveness. One way to do this in a large conference with a protracted time frame is to have the organizers make a long wall chart with one end marked "0 = not so good" and the other end marked "10 = great." As each conference objective is called out, a conference leader with arms held high becomes the "moving needle" along the chart as conferees clap or shout to indicate the degree of success. All participants witness the conference success while enjoying themselves in the process.

The most typical way to evaluate instruction is through a questionnaire given to participants at the conclusion of an event. (An example of a questionnaire is provided in chapter 7, Table 7.5, Workshop Evaluation Form—"Managing Misbehavior in Children.") A questionnaire is a quick and easy way to evaluate participants' impressions of the instruction, although it may not be the most accurate way to do so. Usually evaluation forms are passed out at the end of an event when adults are getting ready to leave and therefore may respond hurriedly. Nonetheless, some valuable information can be gathered. Some areas to evaluate through a questionnaire include

- Goals. To what extent were they achieved?
- Instructional design. Was it effective?
- Instructional content. Did it meet the need?
- Specific methods. Did they work?
- Instructor. What worked, what did not?
- Participant response. Was the experience helpful, enjoyable, and so on?

The following activities will help you evaluate your instructional plan.

Activity 5.1: Photo or video essay

PURPOSE: To provide a visual account of participant accomplishment.

DESCRIPTION: Participants take pictures of their work. These photos, or videos, become a permanent account of their work in the class. This activity promotes creativity and encourages participants to come up with a concrete representation of their work. Participants might use disposable or digital cameras. Participants are asked to accompany their work with verbal or written descriptions or areas for further inquiry.

Activity 5.2: Live demonstrations

PURPOSE: Participants demonstrate learning results.

DESCRIPTION: Participants are asked to provide a concrete example of their new learning. A recital is a common demonstration of musical skill. This approach can be easily adapted to any learning. You are asking participants to show what they learned. Math class participants can put formulas on a blackboard, child care training participants can show how they conduct storytelling to class members, or marketing workshop participants might demonstrate their ad campaign. If a real-world demonstration is not possible, role plays can be used. The audience may be a group of participants or the instructor alone.

Activity 5.3: Journaling

PURPOSE: Journal writing provides a written log of learning.

DESCRIPTION: A journal can be a handy way of recording learning for classroom discussions, instructor evaluations, or future reference by participants. A journal can be simple and short or an extensive and complex record of learning. The format can be index cards used to organize information easily or a book to record the flow of thoughts or events.

Activity 5.4: Group project

PURPOSE: A group project provides for a cooperative evaluation effort.

DESCRIPTION: A group project is a way for participants to work together to show evidence of learning. A group project can be used for a short course or workshop or as the culmination of extended course work. The instructor may want to create conditions so all members of a group contribute equally. The instructor can appoint and meet with participant team leaders to accomplish this or meet periodically with the team to assess how participants are working cooperatively.

Activity 5.5: Image of learning

PURPOSE: This activity uses visual art to communicate learning.

DESCRIPTION: Mind mapping, collages, montages, sculptures, diagrams, and models are examples of visual images that show learning. The image can be evaluated based on well-defined criteria or on reactions that are more subjective. The evaluation can be done by class members or by the instructor.

Activity 5.6: Group testing

PURPOSE: Group testing provides a public evaluation with low risk for participants.

DESCRIPTION: The instructor constructs a short test based on information taught. Then the test is put on an overhead projector, computer projector, or whiteboard. An objective test is best with fill-in answers such as matching or true-and-false questions. The instructor presents the test, and participants can call out answers for a quick check of accuracy. The test can be repeated until the whole class makes a perfect response. Small groups can take a similar test. You can add spice to this technique by offering prizes for correct answers.

Activity 5.7: Participant teachers

PURPOSE: This activity uses teaching to demonstrate ability.

DESCRIPTION: Have participants teach each other a topic or skill as a means of demonstrating their knowledge or ability. You may have different individuals or groups learn different parts of the subject and teach them to others. Alternatively, you may have everyone learn the same thing and then take turns teaching it again to each other. This is a good way to involve participants as teachers and have them evaluate each other.

For more ideas about evaluation, review the learning activities in Systematic Strategy 2, earlier in this chapter. You can adapt these methods of assessment for use as methods of evaluation.

Summary

Remember that your participants will gain much from a program that is well planned, involves the participants in decisions about their learning, and has a logical flow. Evaluation is essential to keep your program effective. The next chapter will help you design instruction that is engaging and challenging for your adult participants.

The Stimulating Instructor Style: Strategies and learning activities

Adults become motivated and learn more when they are challenged with new ideas that are presented in interesting and lively ways. The Stimulating Instructor Style is characterized by provocative presentations that inspire and persuade participants to change their attitudes and behavior. Information is presented in ways that engage participants and make them think. The stimulating strategy and learning activities in this chapter will help you design instruction that is interesting and dynamic and makes an impact on your participants. When instruction is stimulating, lasting positive change is possible.

Stimulating strategies include the following:

- Strategy 6—Present information in interesting, useful ways
- Strategy 7—Use active learning approaches
- Strategy 8—Encourage creativity
- Strategy 9—Help participants solve real problems
- Strategy 10—Help participants practice new learning

Stimulating Strategy 6—Present information in interesting, useful ways

Participants need new perspectives and fresh ways to cope because adults tend to think and act in familiar and rigid patterns. Instructors must challenge adults to change by challenging the old and introducing the new as a valid alternative.

Though lectures can be deadly, instructors commonly use this teaching method to get their ideas across. Lectures are quick and easy. They are *efficient* at getting out a message but may not be the most *effective.* That is, they may not accomplish your goal, which is to create positive change in your participants. Lectures may be effective under certain conditions:

- The topic is vitally important to the audience. For example, if you are riding in a sinking ship and the captain is explaining the best method for disembarking, you very likely will pay close attention and act accordingly.
- The lecturer is so admired or loved that you pay attention out of loyalty and pure devotion. If Elvis returned and spoke to his fans, they would hang on his every word.
- The speaker is so highly charismatic and forceful that the listeners become magically absorbed in wonder and awe. This is rare, but we have all heard such speakers and we are moved and even transformed in those moments.

Combine those three elements and you have one powerful lecture.

Now consider the average adult instructor. We are called upon to teach in our local workplaces, college classes, churches and temples, or community organizations. We hope these organizations are not sinking ships! Calculate the degree to which we are afforded honor and loyalty, and let's face it, we need to do more than just stand up and lecture in order to make a significant impact or effect meaningful change. Even if you are not charismatic or forceful, you want to present your good ideas to participants in ways that will be effective.

The following activities help you present information in useful, interesting ways.

Activity 6.1: The lecturette—a very short lecture

PURPOSE: To present information in a format that is brief and easy to digest.

DESCRIPTION: The lecturette is a short talk that presents the main points or principles to a group. Some key factors in making the lecturette work:

- Conciseness. Make it short, one to fifteen minutes.
- Precision. Provide only the essential information needed to move a group forward.
- Illumination. Offer information that is unique and new to the audience or that sheds new light on the subject or shows a different twist.
- Table. The lecturette should be accompanied by demonstrations, stories, or visual aids to help you show as well as tell.

- Context. The lecturette should fit neatly into a total presentation. It can be used to introduce or summarize an activity. You can use lecturettes in a series, building them to a grand conclusion.

Activity 6.2: Sequencing

PURPOSE: To provide a logical pattern for better understanding and retention.

DESCRIPTION: Pay attention to how you organize your ideas depending on the subject matter and your target audience. Here are some ways to organize your presentations:

- Opening, middle, closing. Lectures or speeches often have this pattern. Begin with an attention-getting opening such as a question, a startling set of facts, or a challenge. The middle part of your presentation should answer the question or respond to the facts or the challenge. The closing summarizes the main point.

- General to specific. You can organize a talk or a whole curriculum with this pattern. Begin with the widest topic and narrow it down to the practical details of the matter. Here is an outline for teaching new child care staff to wash their hands for the sake of good hygiene. It addresses the topic from general to specific information.

  What is a germ?

  Where are germs found?

  What happens when you don't wash?

  Steps in hand washing.

  Practice and test how well you did.

- Simple to complex. Begin with the simplest concepts and move on to more complicated concepts. If you were to teach active listening, you might start with simple skills such as eye contact and posture for better listening. Then move on to more advanced skills such as para-phrasing and summarizing. The next level of complexity might include counseling and consulting.

- The list. Sometimes ideas are organized in a simple list. For example, in a class on techniques for getting acquainted, there are three cate-gories: name games, small-group exercises, and large-group exercises. The instructor just goes down the list in each category (using no special order within the category) describing and demonstrating each one in turn. A list is a good way to organize information you will be presenting.

- Problem solving. Start with problem definition (where we are), next move on to the desired outcomes (where we want to be), and finally lay out the solutions (how to get where we want to be).

- Logic pyramid. Start by presenting your main points; offer supporting evidence for each point in turn; end with a summary. This structure is good when you are trying to teach and persuade an audience.

Activity 6.3: Visual aids

PURPOSE: Visual aids add punch to your teaching points.

DESCRIPTION: Your ideas will stick longer if you add visual reinforcement as you teach. Below is a checklist of ideas.

blackboard or whiteboard

flip chart

wall hangings

displays

demonstrations

videos

photographs

decorations with your theme

handouts

buttons and badges

flowcharts (on paper; on the floor, walls, or ceiling)

overhead projections (slides, transparencies, laptop computer presentations)

physical objects as metaphors

"Show and Tell"

object lessons

drawings

posters

books

electronic projections (computer or Internet projections)

videoconferencing

skits

Activity 6.4: Readings

PURPOSE: Readings present information or directions in written form.

DESCRIPTION: Have you ever thought it would be better to be handed something to read rather than listen to a talk? If you provide handouts that cover the same material you plan to talk about, why not just let participants read it for themselves? Printing material in manageable chunks (list of important points or distinct paragraphs) lets participants absorb the information, discuss it in small groups, and then solicit questions from individuals in the larger group. To expand learning further, let those willing to venture a guess give their answers first and then fill in the blanks or correct errors. You can always answer the toughest questions yourself.

Activity 6.5: Demonstrations

PURPOSE: Demonstrations provide a lesson through words and actions.

DESCRIPTION: A demonstration is a powerful way to teach because it offers a way to learn by seeing and hearing. If people can hear, see, touch, and ask questions, they will retain information better. In a listening workshop, the instructor demonstrates the skills needed for good listening before participants try it. For adults, a demonstration is an advanced form of the "Show and Tell" we recall from our preschool days, and it works just as well with adults as it does with kids.

Activity 6.6: Participants as teachers

PURPOSE: This activity teaches the teacher as well as the participant.

DESCRIPTION: The task of learning information or skills can be divided into steps or separate units that individuals or groups of participants can master. Each person or group becomes an "expert," and then they teach it to other participants. Think of ways to get your participants teaching each other to power up your lessons. Some ideas:

- Assign to a participant the task of learning a portion of your lesson.
- Put portions of the content into the hands of a small group and have them check in with you before teaching it to others.
- Team-teach a topic with participant volunteers.

- Create learning teams whose task it is to share what they learn with each other and work on answering tough questions. The instructor becomes a consultant to the teams.
- Discover who in your workshop or class is already familiar with portions of the topic or has special skills, and let that person teach.
- Facilitate a learning exchange where each small group teaches another small group in turn or they take turns teaching the larger group.

Activity 6.7: Seven best speaking tips

PURPOSE: These tips encourage effective speaking.

DESCRIPTION: Listed below are some important tips for effective speaking.

- Remind yourself constantly that your audience, not you, matters most.
- Conserve words; don't ramble.
- Use good posture, make eye contact, and gesture as you focus on your audience.
- Speak more slowly than seems natural, and project your voice.
- Use appropriate voice inflections and well-planned pauses.
- Overcome nervousness. Use deep breathing or other techniques; wear comfortable clothing that will not show perspiration; simplify hand movements if you are shaky; remind yourself that you have an important message for your audience that they will appreciate.
- Practice. Perfect your timing, sequence, stories, and tables. Rehearse in front of an imaginary audience, a mirror, or some trusted friends.

Stimulating Strategy 7—Use active learning approaches

Experienced instructors know that adults learn by doing, not just sitting and hearing someone talk at them. Variety is the spice of life and learning. Adults should be actively involved in learning tasks at least 50 percent of the time. Use a variety of methods that engage thought, feeling, and all of the senses. Informational presentations should always be balanced with experiential learning.

One model of teaching uses two instructional modes: *action to analysis,* and *analysis to action.* In the action-to-analysis mode, an activity is planned to stimulate thinking, and then participants are guided in gathering principles from the activity. For example, to teach child care providers to recognize quality care, show a video with providers modeling best practices. Ask the participants to take note of similarities among the providers shown. This is the *action.* Next, solicit their discoveries, list them on a flip chart, and discuss them. This is the *analysis.* You will be pleased to find that adult participants will virtually teach themselves in these situations. You simply become a facilitator in the process.

In the analysis-to-action mode, the instructor presents some key ideas and then asks the group to try them out. For example, participants in a listening workshop are taught principles and skills of good listening. After questions are answered and participants understand what is expected, they participate in practice sessions where they can apply what they learned.

Instructors can combine the two instructional modes. For example, after explaining how to listen actively and asking participants to practice the skills (analysis to action) the instructor could ask participants to list some insights and discoveries they made during the practice (action to analysis). This deepens and reinforces learning. Instructional Modes: Instructor and Learner Roles (Table 3-1) presents the roles of the instructor and participants in this model. The Active Teaching Cycle (Table 3-2) presents the same two modes in another format.

Activity 7.1: Movement

Purpose: Movement keeps learning lively.

Description: Get people moving around in the learning space. At first, adults are reluctant to get up and move around. Adults are conditioned to sit still and listen. When asked to move around they may initially resist, so persist. Assign participants to move to another group; or get in pairs, find another pair, discuss, and report. Insist that small-group participants sit close enough so that neighboring small groups will not interfere with discussions.

As an example, in an orientation class for new child care applicants, an instructor helps participants move around while learning about diversity activities for children. She asks small groups of participants to send someone up to

TABLE 3-1

Instructional Modes
Instructor and Learner Roles

ANALYSIS  ACTION

Instructor: teaches, demonstrates, illustrates, or draws from the students the key principles, knowledge, or skills that need to be learned. This can include helping the students find learning resources that teach the basic ideas.

Learner: listens, reads, takes notes, absorbs, contributes ideas, thinks, analyzes, imagines, and so on.

Instructor: creates experiences, organizes field trips, gives instructions, sets up experiments, encourages, guides, and critiques students as they make discoveries about what they learned from the analysis.

Learner: practices, follows directions, experiments, tries out, rehearses, plays with, takes risks, discovers, records, and so on.

ACTION  ANALYSIS

Instructor: creates experiences, sets up experiments, designs activities, provides tools, gives instructions for exploration. The activities should be designed so they naturally lead toward discoveries that help students find significant and relevant answers.

Learner: explores, manipulates, gets involved, tries things out, immerses self in tasks, takes risks, follows directions, keeps alert to new learning, and so on.

Instructor: facilitates discussion, draws out truths from the actions encountered. The teacher helps the learner make sense out of what was experienced by bringing order out of chaos, collating information, or helping students draw conclusions.

Learner: thinks about principles, compares, draws conclusions, ponders, makes lists, writes papers, and so on.

the diversity display table, choose an item, and bring it back to the group. The group then uses the item to stimulate discussion about diversity activities.

You can send small groups to cluster in corners to complete assignments. Label the corners and have people cluster under appropriate labels;

TABLE 3-2

The Active Teaching Cycle

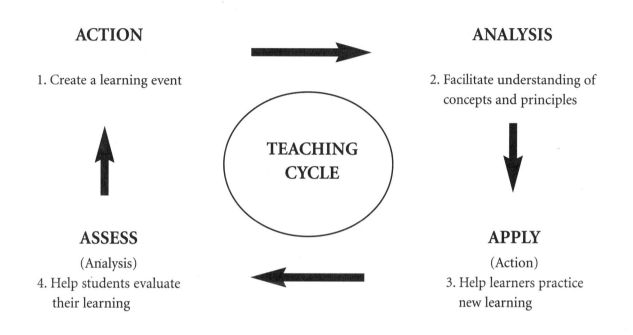

ACTION

1. Create a learning event

ANALYSIS

2. Facilitate understanding of concepts and principles

TEACHING CYCLE

ASSESS

(Analysis)

4. Help students evaluate their learning

APPLY

(Action)

3. Help learners practice new learning

change the labels; and start again. Remember that adults will initially balk at moving around; when the class is over, however, they will thank you for getting them moving.

Activity 7.2: Debate

PURPOSE: Debate helps participants learn through active persuasion.

DESCRIPTION: People disagree when participating in learning experiences. Why not formalize the disagreement and stage a debate? Choose a topic and let participants line up on one side or another. The side a person takes is not as important as his ability to use newly learned information gained in the process of debating. What will make your case most effective? What facts do you need? What opinions are being presented? What is the basic premise? Participants can caucus with a supportive group, formulate a plan, and then challenge the opposing team.

Activity 7.3: Participant demonstrations

PURPOSE: Participant demonstrations make participants responsible for an activity.

DESCRIPTION: Participants can make posters, put on skits, and create displays to demonstrate new learning. Have props ready for individuals or groups to use. If you teach a skill, you will find demonstrations invaluable. A good pattern to follow is to tell them how, show them how, and then let participants demonstrate. Follow up with a debriefing session.

Activity 7.4: Case studies or scenarios

PURPOSE: This activity teaches by working on sample problems.

DESCRIPTION: This is a classic way to engage participants. Written scenarios or case studies help participants begin to understand and manipulate the real world safely. Show a picture of a playground and see if child care workers can spot the health or safety hazards. Create a fictional story or a real example about a child care worker who has to handle a difficult behavior situation, and let participants work on solutions. First, teach a method for handling certain situations. Next, ask participants to apply the new method to a case study.

Activity 7.5: Drama and role play

PURPOSE: Dramatic simulations help teach.

DESCRIPTION: Drama is fun for some, not for others. Those who like drama should be allowed to express themselves. Dramas need audiences, so do not force everyone to be actors. People can also be live props or help set the scene.

Two or three participants can stage a role play without having to face an audience. Set the scene, specify the behavior you want dramatized, and then let small groups work on their own. The instructor can wander around the room and act as a consultant. Some groups may volunteer to perform their role play for others, but it is not necessary that they do so.

Activity 7.6: Small groups and intergroup sharing

PURPOSE: Sharing uses dialogue to teach.

DESCRIPTION: Give a small group of adults an interesting topic to discuss and they will get involved quickly. Wrestling with ideas and concepts in a small group encourages learning from each other. You can follow up with small groups reporting their discoveries. Mix and match groups. Start with pairs, join pairs, and then join these to form groups of eight. Discuss a topic or work on a problem, and then reverse the process. You can switch pairs and then start all over again.

Stimulating Strategy 8—Encourage creativity

Adults should be engaged in creating and experimenting with new knowledge to foster change and growth. Help them invent, originate, conceive, author, and express their creative side by removing fear and ambivalence. Present a process that helps adults take the creative risk.

Instructors can help adults become creative by providing a framework in which they feel free to explore options. Family child care providers will find it easier to think of creative learning activities when they are given categories to guide their creative thinking. For example, they might be asked to think of ways to help a child learn new words, learn how to solve problems, learn how to get along, and so forth. The participants, armed with a list of categories as a guide, come up with their own ideas. In other words, the instructor provides the categories, and the participants provide the originality and creative thinking.

Creativity is the active use of imagination to produce something unique. It goes beyond painting a picture or composing music. It means drawing on your inner resources to produce a new thought or point of view, an artistic representation, an idea, or a solution to a problem. We all have an urge to create in some form or another. As adults, we tend to be creatures of habit and routine, but we are all quite capable of exploring, inventing, and improving our world. Adult participants need to affirm their own creative powers in problem solving and artistic expression.

When we learn, we reinvent ourselves—our behavior, knowledge, and understanding. The very act of learning, therefore, is creative. Adult instructors have a unique opportunity to facilitate the process of creative transformation in participants. Allowing adults to invent, originate, conceive, author, and imagine aids in learning, change, and growth. The relationship between creativity and learning is summarized in How the Creative Process Aids Learning (Table 3-3).

TABLE 3-3

How the Creative Process Aids Learning

While being creative adults become more:	because creativity...
involved	...draws one fully into an activity
wakeful	...calls for complete attention
energized	...makes one feel alive
aware	...heightens one's sensitivity
flexible	...causes one to drop old ways of doing things
positive	...is hopeful and friendly
focused	...calls for sustained attention
daring	...calls one to adventure and to take risks
delighted	...is enjoyable
childlike	...makes one feel young
reachable	...opens one up to new experience and ideas
inventive	...causes one to make new connections

The following activities can be used to support participants' creativity.

Activity 8.1: Remembering

PURPOSE: This activity helps adults recall their creative moments.

DESCRIPTION: Provide a definition of creativity such as this: "Being creative means drawing on your inner resources or your imagination to bring about something new. This can result in a pleasing photograph, a work of art, a unique solution to a problem, or an idea that makes others stop and rethink what they are doing." Based on this definition, ask participants to recall one or two incidents when they were creative as children or as adults. (Instructors may want to share some examples from their own creative past.) Have them think of what conditions surrounded those incidents. Next, participants should share with a partner or small group. Collect these moments on a flip chart and see what the group discovers about their patterns of creativity. Most people have forgotten some wonderful examples of being creative. As you ask this group to be creative in your session, you will have plenty of evidence to encourage them.

Activity 8.2: Provide tools for creativity

PURPOSE: Providing the right tools gives participants what they need to be creative.

DESCRIPTION: A tool is, simply, a means to an end. More precisely, tools are the necessary materials, instructions, techniques, or instruments needed to perform some task, in this case to create something. Examples of tools are a paintbrush for a painter, a map for a treasure hunter, or construction blocks for a child care provider. If you are going to facilitate creativity, you must carefully think through and provide all the tools necessary for the task. Here's a sample list of tools:

> clear instructions for your participants
>
> enough supplies for everyone
>
> backing material—paper, poster board
>
> adhesives—tape, glue
>
> art materials—paint, pencils, clay
>
> miscellaneous—paper, magazines, beads, string
>
> sufficient space for working—table surfaces, floor space
>
> surfaces—protective covering for tables, floors, etc.
>
> scripts—scenarios, role descriptions
>
> resources—reference books, song books, idea stimulators

Activity 8.3: Provide a clear example

PURPOSE: Samples help participants get started.

DESCRIPTION: When adults are first challenged to be inventive and creative, it helps them to have some examples of what they are reaching for. This might be called a "vision of quality." If you ask participants to write a cooperative group poem, read one of yours or provide samples from other groups. If you ask for an idea to be presented as a collage, have one prepared to show. Because adults will tend to rely on replicating your example instead of stretching themselves for the truly novel, emphasize that all participant work must be completely original. Once a work is done, however, never criticize participants' attempts at creativity—remember that it's tough for many adults to express creativity.

To provide a vision of quality, you should show, demonstrate, or describe an example in the most vivid way possible so participants have some idea of what to aim for. In a drawing class, the instructor first lets participants see the works of art by the masters with explanations of the principles of their work that could be practiced by the participants. Novice artists are not destined to become masters but need a vision of what they hope to accomplish. When showing child care providers how to teach, your own instructional approach becomes a model.

Activity 8.4: Set clear boundaries

PURPOSE: Clear boundaries promote freedom by setting limits.

DESCRIPTION: Paradoxically, boundaries help us feel free—this is strange but true. The canvas for the artist sets a parameter. The lump of clay, just so big, limits the potter. When you ask participants to create new ideas, it is helpful to suggest limits such as limiting the number of ideas ("Think of three ways to improve your child care center") or limiting the time ("You have three minutes to come up with a new plan"). Besides providing boundaries, setting limits challenges participants to focus their efforts. And it adds to the fun.

Some ways instructors set boundaries to encourage creativity include the following:

- Time limits. "Your group has just ten minutes to work."
- Space limits. "Use only what you find in this room to create a role play."
- Subject or topic limits. "Groups one and two are to think of ways to prevent problems, and groups three and four are to think of ways to solve them."
- Thematic limits. "Create a poem about a toddler's eating habits."
- Limit the size of work groups. "Get into groups of five and . . ."
- Simplify the task. "Create a song using the tune of . . ."
- Limit the number of responses. "Think of ten ideas to improve your job."
- Limit the number of steps in a process. "One, think of a feeling. Two, select colored pens that depict that feeling. Three, draw the feeling any way you like. Four, show and tell it to your partner."

- Limit the number of elements to manipulate. "Select one action word and act it out."
- Limit the purpose. "Think of some new ways to help parents feel confident about their child care skills."

Activity 8.5: Encourage the creative risk

PURPOSE: Risk taking helps adults overcome the fear of failure when creating.

DESCRIPTION: The fear of failure that adults associate with being creative is often based on experience. Fear of ridicule can be a powerful deterrent to creative efforts. This fear looms large, particularly when participants are asked to share their efforts with others. The most effective way to encourage participants is to assure them that failure and ridicule will not occur. The least effective way is to try to push or persuade adults to perform. Set the tone for creativity with these assurances:

- The goal of the activity is not to learn to perform wonders. This is not a test of creative potential. It is only a means to an end.
- Creativity is a process, not a product. It is a process of generation-reaction-regeneration. It is not a once-and-for-all event.
- There are no wrong answers in a creative exercise. A vision of quality is not a measure of success. It is simply a launching pad for the creative process.
- The instructor will not judge participants, and others should follow your model of acceptance and respect for everyone's efforts. In learning, there is a time for evaluation, but the time for creativity should be judgment-free.
- A learning environment is a place to experiment.
- Participants and instructors form a learning community, which is characterized by mutual support. Effective learning takes place as we work together to gain skill, knowledge, and understanding.

Activity 8.6: Share and celebrate creativity

PURPOSE: This activity reinforces creative efforts.

DESCRIPTION: When adult participants stretch themselves to be creative, they deserve some recognition. Create opportunities to share the results with others and celebrate. This can be simple or elaborate depending on the circumstance. Here are some ideas for sharing and celebrating:

- Ask a person from each group of participants to report to the whole class.
- Have small groups take turns showing or demonstrating their creative work.
- Help each group set up a station and ask groups to circulate and view them all.
- Suggest that each individual show and tell about her work to a subgroup or to the whole class.
- Ask each group to pass its work around the room for appreciation.
- Make a video presentation for all to watch.
- Create a display encompassing the whole class's effort for outsiders.
- Publish a class paper using participant work.
- Create a photo display.
- Encourage the whole class to cheer and applaud heartily after group or individual reports are made.
- Give prizes to all participants or for certain qualities of a presentation (most lively, colorful, daring, ambitious, and so on).
- Have a party!

Activity 8.7: Four phases of creativity

PURPOSE: This activity uses a process to enhance creativity.

DESCRIPTION: One way of thinking about creativity is in these four phases: reflect, release, receive, and respond. You can prepare participants for creative activities by allowing time for them to go through each creative phase.

- Reflect. Reflection involves relaxing, quieting and centering one's mind, calming, and becoming silent to allow the creative thought process to begin. Some methods for reflection include deep breathing, meditation, guided imagery, journaling, and quiet conversation.
- Release. This step involves letting go of distractions such as worries, cares, and day-to-day concerns. This is the time to free oneself from

prescribed methods and past patterns and liberate the mind to see things in new ways. Some methods include writing, mentally letting go of all thoughts, and invigorating exercise.

- Receive. Now is the time to allow new ideas to flow in. This step involves free-associating, exploring, sorting, choosing, and structuring thoughts and ideas. This is the nitty-gritty process of discovering the novel idea or fresh viewpoint. Some methods include brainstorming, listing, free-associating, experimenting, discussing, mind-mapping, questioning, trying out words, storytelling, and testing.

- Respond. This is when the ideas are expressed. Now is the time to make the decision, sling the paint, or sing the song. Try out the new solution, either in simulation or under real conditions. Some methods include creating a work of art, constructing, writing, and performing.

Stimulating Strategy 9—Help participants solve real problems

Adults should be engaged in solving important and relevant problems. Problem-solving techniques can be taught and used to reinforce the course content. Encourage participants to work on decisions or issues that they face in their daily lives.

Participants are motivated when they are solving problems that are important to them. In an orientation class for people applying to be state-licensed family child care providers, invite successful providers to come and speak about the problems and possibilities they will face in the real world. The participants will see the procedural information they got from the trainers in a new light. ("I can apply this to my situation.")

When participants are engaged in solving problems, they actively think and manipulate the new understanding, knowledge, and skills they are learning. This kind of engagement increases the effectiveness and enjoyment of learning.

The following activities will help you give participants real problems to solve.

Activity 9.1: Active listening

PURPOSE: Active listening helps participants learn about and solve problems.

DESCRIPTION: You can use this method with participants grouped in threes or in pairs. With a group of three you will have a listener, speaker, and observer with rotating roles. The speaker shares a problem, while the listener uses active listening skills. As the listener listens and facilitates the speaker's reflections, solutions begin to emerge. Finally, the observer joins the conversation and the group attempts to articulate a final and best solution.

This process works well with partners too. Each participant takes a turn as listener and a turn as speaker. The listener takes notes, which are shared with the speaker, and they discuss the content of the sharing as well as feelings and reactions during the session.

Activity 9.2: Participant consultants

PURPOSE: This teaches by facilitating a solution.

DESCRIPTION: After presenting a topic or skill, the instructor divides the class into "clients" and "consultants." The instructor presents case problems to the clients (or participants describe real problems they face), and the consultants assist them in working toward solutions based on the lesson. Next, the clients and consultants switch roles with new problems to solve. The instructor may want to devise some special instructions for the consultants or provide a guide sheet for both roles to follow.

Activity 9.3: Like-minded meetings

PURPOSE: To motivate problem solving as people with similar interests join forces.

DESCRIPTION: The instructor asks participants who have a special interest in a problem to work together. In an instructor training workshop, for example, time is provided for groups of participants to work on solutions to problems, such as how to handle participants who are resistant or angry or those who are too talkative. The small groups report their solutions to the larger group. A variation on this is to have people who have no interest in the problem work on the solution, which adds the dimension of objectivity and expands the learning of those who might otherwise miss an opportunity.

Activity 9.4: Problem-solving teams

PURPOSE: Team effort provides long-term problem solving.

DESCRIPTION: The problem-solving team is a group that stays together and works on a particular problem over an extended period. This may be an all-day team in a workshop or a collaboration among participants outside of the workshop who come back together after a period of time to report results. The team studies the problem in depth and then makes periodic reports or a final report.

Activity 9.5: Help exchange

PURPOSE: To encourage participants to share problems and find quick solutions.

DESCRIPTION: Individuals or small groups write out specific problems they want help with, and then the problems are passed from group to group with solutions added to the paper as it progresses. The originator receives the list of solutions at the end of the round. Originators of each problem can discuss the range of solutions and select the best ones to try out.

Activity 9.6: Symbolic or simulated problem solving

PURPOSE: This exercise uses simulations and games to solve problems.

DESCRIPTION: Real problems can be simulated, allowing participants to apply new learning. Here are some exercises:

- Act out scenarios. Participants act out problem situations for participants to solve.
- Case studies. Common problems are presented in written form.
- Puzzles. Puzzles and games simulate real problems. (Redesign board games to fit your topic, make puzzle pieces that symbolize topics, pose riddles that help participants recall new learning, and so on.)

Activity 9.7: Circle of advice

PURPOSE: This activity helps participants share answers with the whole group.

DESCRIPTION: Participants sit in a circle. Problems are brought before the group and those in the circle take turns presenting solutions. Circle participants may present a solution or pass if they wish. Follow this with a small-group discussion on what was learned.

Stimulating Strategy 10—Help participants practice new learning

Participants should be able to try out new behaviors, so it is important to provide a way for them to practice and receive feedback on the concepts or strategies being taught. They need an opportunity to rehearse strategies that they may be called upon to perform in the future. This strategy is similar to the rehearsal for an actor. The goal of rehearsal is to be prepared when the curtain goes up, just as participants need to be prepared for roles in life and work.

Learning should be like entering a refuge or shelter where you are free to make mistakes. You are gently guided into becoming more proficient, competent, knowledgeable, or wise. In a learning role, you are protected. Nevertheless, this refuge must prepare you for the real world.

After those who care for children have spent time in a workshop, they will return to the home or classroom setting where each moment counts. Even if just for an hour, the workshop should be a safe haven in which participants can prepare to face the awesome responsibility to come.

The following activities will help participants practice their new learning.

Activity 10.1: Plan, write, and review

PURPOSE: This activity provides conceptual practice.

DESCRIPTION: After teaching concepts, ask participants to make specific plans that describe how they will apply the new ideas in their lives or work roles. Participants write out these plans and then share them with a partner, a small group, or the whole class for review and critique.

Activity 10.2: Demonstrate using skill standards

PURPOSE: This activity uses standards to guide practice.

DESCRIPTION: Participants may want and need to be able to demonstrate specific levels of competence to ensure that learning has been mastered. Some ways to set up this practice include the following:

- The instructor can observe participants and assess their performance.
- Participants can be trained to assess each other's performance.
- Small groups can practice until all members reach a given level of competence.

- A panel of judges made up of participants or experts can be used for assessments that are more subjective.

Activity 10.3: Video feedback

PURPOSE: Use immediate video feedback to objectify practice.

DESCRIPTION: Being observed with a camera so you can see your mistakes and successes adds potency to the experience. Seeing ourselves as others see us brings an element of reality to practice. Sitting down with a mentor or a coach to look at the video helps participants hone skills. A series of video sessions is better than a single exposure. Schedule these knowing that this process can be very time consuming.

Activity 10.4: Practitioner/expert review

PURPOSE: Use experienced practitioners to assist with rehearsal.

DESCRIPTION: Send participants out to practitioners, or bring practitioners into the classroom to review participant practice sessions. An effective way to practice good child caring or supervisory skills is to do so in the company of those who already have the skills and can critique the participant. Many practitioners are willing and eager to do this as a service to their field.

Activity 10.5: Field work

PURPOSE: Fieldwork provides on-the-job training.

DESCRIPTION: This has been a classic way of providing practice in many fields. Participants are asked to do the real job with a mentor or under observation in a setting where the work really takes place. It is important to remember for classroom or field instructors that the goal is instruction, not production.

Activity 10.6: Small group of peers

PURPOSE: These groups provide safety in numbers when practicing skills.

DESCRIPTION: Learning teams or small, temporary support groups can ease the tension while practicing. The goal for these small groups is to help each member become as knowledgeable and proficient as possible. An element of friendly competition can be added to increase the fun and motivation.

When the group feels that each member is ready, it demonstrates for the whole class.

Activity 10.7: Rehearsal or role play

Purpose: This activity simulates real life.

Description: Role-playing should be used with great care. Many adults fear the name because they have been forced to act in front of a large group. It is best to use role play in small groups with the control held by the participants. Always allow adult participants a choice about role-playing. Here is a suggested method:

1. Prepare and deliver a clear definition of the skills that participants will practice.
2. Demonstrate the skills.
3. Divide participants into the smallest group units possible.
4. Allow small groups to select roles, practice, and assess their own members.
5. Act as a roving consultant and facilitator.

Summary

Adult participants learn more and have more fun learning when you use the strategies and learning activities from the Stimulating Instructor Style. Instruction that challenges adult participants helps them solve real-life problems, engages them actively, and encourages them to strive for greater understanding, knowledge, and skills. In the next chapter you will learn some ways to add the elements of surprise, fun, and creativity to your instruction.

The Spontaneous Instructor Style: Strategies and learning activities

Spontaneous instruction gives adults the opportunity and permission to try out new ways of seeing and learn to break free from old patterns. Unpredictability fosters the process of "unfreezing" adults from the same old line of thinking. Plan and allow for play, humor, and surprise in your instruction. When adults play, laugh, and take risks together, the walls of resistance weaken and fall. This chapter presents the spontaneous strategies and learning activities that help you design instruction to liberate your participants from standard ways of understanding and behaving. When instruction is spontaneous, anything can happen, which frees not only the participant but the instructor as well.

Spontaneous strategies include the following:
- Strategy 11—Help participants tell their stories
- Strategy 12—Make it funny, make it fun
- Strategy 13—Use imagination and the arts
- Strategy 14—Build in risk taking
- Strategy 15—Take time to reflect

Spontaneous Strategy 11—Help participants tell their stories

Adults like to hear and tell stories. Much learning can take place as participants share their stories and experiences. The adult instructor should facilitate this exchange, because it leads to practical solutions for problems in life and work. Structure the session so that a significant portion of the course content flows from these interactions.

Use small groups in your instruction. A smaller audience often allows adults to tell their stories more comfortably. Once you get them started, it is hard to get them to stop. Telling stories is an ancient means of passing on wisdom: "How did you solve the problem I now face?" and "Where did you find a resource?" You can expand your instruction by letting participants share their valuable knowledge. In fact, adults often come to training sessions just to meet and talk with others who share similar situations.

The reason this strategy fits with the spontaneous style is that it adds a measure of unpredictability to instruction. Instructors may guide and direct these encounters hoping for significant insight, learning, and change, but we cannot fully know the result.

The following activities help unearth participants' stories.

Activity 11.1: Small groups

PURPOSE: This activity guides instructors in the use of small groups.

DESCRIPTION: The ideal group size is a matter of debate among facilitators. The best size for close, intimate interaction is three members. The maximum size for discussion groups should be five or six, depending on the task and the time frame. Larger groups need more time to process and involve all members. A group of three allows all participants to take part. When the group size exceeds six, some members of the group will begin to take a strong lead and others will start to fade into the woodwork.

Activity 11.2: Small groups over a longer time

PURPOSE: Using small groups for a long time period stresses the value of groups' staying together.

DESCRIPTION: Small groups are powerful units for learning. To make them more effective, keep small groups meeting together over an extended period rather than having participants switch frequently. Trust created through interaction over longer periods of time provides a greater opportunity for mutual teaching and learning. This emotional closeness combined with mutual work usually results in positive learning.

Activity 11.3: Seating close together

PURPOSE: Physical closeness helps members interact more freely.

DESCRIPTION: When you begin small-group activities, ask participants to get into a small circle and try to "touch knees." This physical closeness may meet with some resistance, so use good judgment, but communicate the importance of direct, close interaction. Point out that being close reduces the interference from conversation in other groups nearby.

Do your best to prevent groups from sitting in a line; in this formation, people on the ends are left out and mentally drift away. Groups seated at tables work well if you use writing materials, but it is preferable to get people together without any physical barriers. Having flexible seating helps, but you can create good personal connections in large auditoriums with rigid seating if participants turn toward people in front or behind them or move to open spaces for conversation.

Activity 11.4: Adult life experiences teach

PURPOSE: This activity promotes the value of adult participants' life experience and knowledge.

DESCRIPTION: Instructors are wise to acknowledge the great wealth of knowledge, expertise, and wisdom of participants. Even if we unwisely decide we want only our own ideas expressed, adult participants filter them through their own experience anyway and reject what does not fit. Here are some reasons to use the prior knowledge and skill of the participants in the teaching process.

- Participants' ideas are tried and true. Participant knowledge and skills are valuable because they come from the world of experience. Often the ideas have been tried and tested, which gives them potency.
- Participants' ideas can reinforce the instructor's points. Even if ideas from participants are not quite accurate, the discussion led by the instructor to get correct information increases everyone's learning.
- Participants' ideas add variety and depth. The comments of other participants are often a welcome relief after spending much time listening to just one person's point of view.
- Exchanging ideas helps everyone enjoy the learning more. The exchange of ideas is fun and profitable. Even a good argument leaves us tingling and alive.
- The exchange adds a greater sense of ownership by the participants. Empowered participants are better participants.

- The exchange increases effectiveness and efficiency of instruction. When we delegate, collaborate, and cooperate we get more for the energy expended.
- Peer opinions are credible. The opinions of one's peers are often more credible than even those of the instructor. The smart instructor uses the power of peer influence for the good of learning.

Activity 11.5: Seven ways to use adult life experience and knowledge

PURPOSE: Brings adults' life experience and knowledge into the classroom.

DESCRIPTION: The normal give-and-take while learning provides grist for the mill among adults. When ideas are flowing, participants will automatically select which ones fit and which ones do not. Here are some more structured ways to use the wisdom of adult participants:

- Know your group. Assess the knowledge and experience of the participants by asking what they know and do not know about the topic. You can use an in-class survey, a pretest, or a verbal inquiry to accomplish this.
- Use small groups. Small discussion or work groups provide an opportunity for participants to share wisdom.
- Let participants present information. Formal or informal presentations by participants, when they are given adequate time to prepare, will enrich the group's experience. The instructor can either stand aside or facilitate these presentations.
- Ask participants to demonstrate. Demonstrations by participants to support class content can add considerable depth in learning. A demonstration is an adult version of "Show and Tell" and is an effective way to teach through practical applications or examples of principles.
- Ask participants to serve as consultants and mentors. Participants can become consultants or mentors to each other. This takes careful matching between participants with expertise and those who need guidance.
- Ask participants to tutor one another. More experienced and advanced participants can tutor those who are less experienced. Tutors

can be assigned or can volunteer to help. Tutoring can be offered when participants request it, or everyone can take turns being a tutor.

- Turn questions back to the group. An easy and effective way to glean the wisdom from a group is to turn questions back to the group. When a participant asks a question, you can defer to the class by asking, "Does anyone have an answer for this problem?"

Activity 11.6: Reaction groups

PURPOSE: Reaction groups allow participants to systematically respond to content.

DESCRIPTION: After each presentation, you can ask participants to form reaction groups to respond to the input. These can meet for just a few minutes or for a longer time. After reactions, let anyone share what they discovered.

Activity 11.7: Guided interaction

PURPOSE: Guided interaction facilitates storytelling.

DESCRIPTION: The instructor may want to structure the interaction to help participants get started. Sentence completions are a good way to do that. Read a sentence, and then ask each person in turn to finish the sentence. Some samples: When I first enter a new group I feel . . . ; In my opinion the best child care provider is one who . . . ; The best teacher I ever had was . . . ; and so on.

Another way to get participants to share stories is to call out subjects and ask individuals in small groups to share any story they know about the topic. Topics might include child safety/child accidents, first child care job, first parent contact, and so on.

Spontaneous Strategy 12—Make it funny, make it fun

Opportunities for playfulness encourage adults to laugh and enjoy themselves. Use and promote humor that facilitates learning, is in good taste, is appropriate to the task, and matches participant values. Encourage surprise, serendipity, and fun in the learning encounter.

Some principles for using humor in teaching adults:

- Never use humor that might ridicule any person, group, or culture. A good test is to imagine telling it to people who are the object of a humorous comment or a joke. Would they accept it, embrace it, and see it as funny? When humor hurts, it creates defensiveness and hinders growth.

- Avoid off-color or sexist jokes. Much adult humor is of this type, but it can stifle the creative spirit. Strive for humor that creates a dynamic, positive flow.
- Use humor that fits your style. When you try to be funny in ways that are not natural, it can fall flat. If you use dry humor, develop and use it. If you tend to forget the punch line, avoid telling jokes.
- Let the group discover what's funny. Most groups you teach have a general sense of what is appropriate humor, so take your cues from them.
- Use humor that directly relates to the topic or enhances learning. Use jokes to introduce a topic or make a point that teaches. Example: "Here's an oxymoron: *childproof.* It could be an interesting way to introduce the need for supervision of kids, because nothing is *childproof.*"
- Use humor indirectly. Use it to put people at ease, to help people get acquainted, and to build relationships.

Some people are better than others at telling jokes. You may be one of those whose timing is off and no one laughs. Others do better with well-timed ad-libs. Use the kind of humor that fits you, but the important thing is to permit and promote humor because it creates a wonderfully charged atmosphere for learning. How Humor Aids Learning (Table 4-1) outlines the many ways that humor asserts a positive influence on the learning experience.

TABLE 4-1

How Humor Aids Learning

Humor relaxes people.

Humor puts people in a good mood to learn.

Humor opens the mind.

Humor awakens. It opens the air passages and blood vessels.

Humor builds rapport. If you laugh with someone, the barriers go down.

Humor invites participation by raising the positive energy level.

Humor warms us up and keeps us alert.

Humor dissipates fears; it disarms our defenses.

Humor is known to aid in healing and wholeness.

Humor makes difficult tasks easier—"a spoonful of sugar helps the medicine go down."

Humor helps make a point stick in the mind. Laugh and it lasts.

The following activities will help you add humor to classes and presentations.

Activity 12.1: Surprises

PURPOSE: Surprises promote humor.

DESCRIPTION: A favorite warm-up is to have people tell their life stories to each other in one minute. Participants often laugh in surprise when they hear the assignment. Surprise gifts, unusual decorations, quirky activities, or unique noises that signal a change in activity add a touch of humor and humanness.

Activity 12.2: The class clown

PURPOSE: Participants with a good sense of humor thrive.

DESCRIPTION: Participants who have a keen sense of humor often add greatly to the class or workshop. They are usually the ones with high social intelligence who know when comic relief is needed. Off-the-cuff humor, side comments, and puns break up potential monotony and keep things light. You can communicate acceptance of such antics through your own smiles and laughter.

Activity 12.3: Anecdotes and stories

PURPOSE: Learning is promoted through humorous stories.

DESCRIPTION: People remember stories. Funny stories are told repeatedly—what a way to make learning last. You can read stories, tell them, or elicit them from the participants. "Does anyone have a story to tell about . . ." (See activity 11.7: Guided Interaction for some topic ideas.)

Activity 12.4: Skits, stunts, and drama

PURPOSE: Use skits, stunts, and drama to promote humor in learning.

DESCRIPTION: Once adults feel comfortable with each other, they will create wonderfully funny skits and drama. Both actors and audiences enjoy it. A teaching topic can come alive when it is dramatized for all to experience. Stunts can be used to loosen people up and get them laughing as they test their dexterity. Challenge participants to show some unique talent they have (curling their tongue, wiggling their ears, crossing their eyes, and so on). These antics elicit spontaneous laughter and quickly loosen things up; an added benefit is that child care professionals see immediate application in their work with children.

Activity 12.5: Songs and chants

PURPOSE: Use songs and chants to promote humor in learning.

DESCRIPTION: Funny songs or chants with motions get people to move, breathe, and laugh. Individuals or small groups can compose songs or invent chants to share right on the spot. The instructor can lead songs or chants to get things started.

Activity 12.6: Games and activities

PURPOSE: Use games and activities to promote humor.

DESCRIPTION: Games and activities are a sure way to get participants to lighten up. Table games, interactive games, active team games, or contests help people have fun and laugh. Gear the types of games to your audience and be ready with several alternatives.

Spontaneous Strategy 13—Use imagination and the arts

Participants should experience creative expression, which fosters positive change. Employ aspects of the arts (visual arts, music, poetry, drama, and so on) that enhance exploration and learning. Encourage participants to use the arts to stretch beyond limits of understanding, knowledge, and skill.

Creative arts awaken our emotions, give us pause, startle us, and bring us gently or starkly to points of change. Art and imagination contain elements of unpredictability and surprise, two characteristics that make them excellent teaching tools suitable for the Spontaneous Instructor Style.

The following activities will bring imagination and the arts into your teaching.

Activity 13.1: Music and singing

PURPOSE: To support spontaneity through music.

DESCRIPTION: Have music playing when participants arrive at your workshop or class. You may want to select music to set a certain mood (light and happy, calming, and so on) or to fit the theme of your instruction. Keep a variety of music from which to choose. Participants can learn by singing songs too. You may have a theme song or make up words to a tune that emphasize your point. If you teach them the words, they will go away humming your lesson all day. Take the time to teach it. You can use songs that small groups make up to summarize what participants have learned. Ask each group to sing their special composition as a way to wrap up the session.

Activity 13.2: Dance and creative movement

PURPOSE: To support spontaneity through dance and creative movement.

DESCRIPTION: Dance or movement can be used as warm-up exercises and to open the mind for learning. Simple circle dances draw a group together. For example, a song and accompanying movement that weaves a group together can be used to teach the importance of community and teamwork. The group forms a line holding hands, and as the music is played or sung, the leader pulls the line along into a weaving that gets tighter and tighter. If the movement is simple and fits the theme, most participants will join in and enjoy it. Let those who don't wish to participate stand aside and clap or encourage others.

Activity 13.3: Drama

PURPOSE: To support spontaneity through drama.

DESCRIPTION: Use role plays and skits to demonstrate learning. Small groups can be assigned topics to use as tables. Some trainers hire professional actors to act out roles of clients, kids, or parents, which allows participants to practice interpersonal skills in a near-real setting. Drama can also be used as a catalyst for discussion. You can use participant-actors to portray scenes that touch the audience's emotions and intellect as a way to spark discussion and enhance learning.

To help participants feel more comfortable, let them practice their roles sufficiently or use small groups for role play. If some participants like to act, allow them to act in most of the dramas you wish to use to demonstrate key ideas.

Activity 13.4: Painting and drawing

PURPOSE: To support spontaneity through painting and drawing.

DESCRIPTION: Painting and drawing can be done individually or in small groups. Murals can be drawn or painted to express part of the learning theme. You can use paintings and drawings by artists in overhead slides or computer projections to illustrate points or stimulate discussion. Individual participants can be asked to create drawings to portray ideas or feelings on the theme of the class. You may want to provide participants with small drawing pads to encourage doodling so they can visually conceptualize ideas during the class. At the end of the workshop, ask participants to share their doodles as a way to summarize the workshop content.

Activity 13.5: Calligraphy and printing

PURPOSE: To support spontaneity through calligraphy and printing.

DESCRIPTION: If you have the talent, you can create signs, posters, and flip charts that are printed nicely. Participants can make their own signs with a little instruction on how it is done. These take-home signs can be used as reminders of things learned. Even one-word reminders on cards can be helpful.

Activity 13.6: Collage

PURPOSE: To support spontaneity through collage.

DESCRIPTION: Collages are popular because they are so easy and fun to do. With a little encouragement, participants will make use of all kinds of materials to express ideas and concepts that they are learning. You need some backing (cardboard, construction paper), glue or tape, magazines, and a variety of small objects such as ribbon, stickers, colored paper, and so on. Be clear about the theme so participants can select appropriate pictures and items to add to the collage.

Activity 13.7: Poetry, haiku, and limericks

PURPOSE: To support spontaneity through poetry.

DESCRIPTION: Read or recite poems to participants as a catalyst for getting participants to think and react. Poetry awakens feelings. Assign poetry writing in journals or as readings to stimulate creative thought. Limericks are easy and can be created by participants on themes or topics being taught.

Haiku poems are created in three lines. The first line uses five syllables, the second uses seven syllables, and the third line uses five syllables. The third line is the "punch line" that drives your point home. Haiku poems do not rhyme. You may need to provide instruction on writing and performing haiku, but these short, pithy poems can be very moving. Here is a haiku the author wrote while teaching English in China:

My Chinese students
Wait in silence for my words
West, East meet right here.

A good way to remember facts is to rhyme them. Make it a class assignment for each person or small group to write a rhyming poem on some aspect of the class content. To remind adult participants to know their purpose before speaking, they were taught this potent little rhyme:

Before you speak,
Know just what you desire:
Do you want to inform, inquire?
Influence or inspire?

Spontaneous Strategy 14—Build in risk taking

To promote an attitude of risk taking, instructors must model this attitude for participants. You must be willing to change and grow yourself. Communicate, through an appropriate level of self-disclosure, the humanness of us all.

Appropriately sharing your own life and struggles is a risk that teaches participants to do the same. The instructor also needs to model an acceptance of trial and error by participants in the classroom.

You must be willing to create situations where participants move beyond their usual responses. Mostly we want to stay safe and warm in our cocoons, but the instructor's role is to unravel the cocoon and invite participants to experience something different.

The following activities will help participants take risks.

Activity 14.1—Meet new people

PURPOSE: Meeting new people promotes risk taking through get-acquainted exercises.

DESCRIPTION: Workshops and classes put us in a position to meet new people. Too often, instructors do not allow participants to meet each other and "mix it up." Make it a normal part of your instructional routine to get people talking to one another. Rather than the typical exercise of asking participants to say their names and where they are from, ask them to share some important things about themselves with at least one other participant. This is where risk taking begins.

Activity 14.2—Self-disclosure

PURPOSE: Self-disclosure promotes risk taking.

DESCRIPTION: Make it your practice to get people to disclose some things about themselves with others early in the workshop. Because adults are often uncomfortable or afraid to talk about their own lives, try to make it fun and easy to do. One simple and practically foolproof way of doing this is to divide the class into pairs or groups of three or four participants. Ask that each person answer the question "What's on your plate, personally or professionally?" (Make sure participants know that this is an optional exercise.) With that one little question, adult participants will immediately begin to talk freely. It is a great opportunity to take a self-disclosure risk and have someone listen to you in the process. It provides an opportunity to tell as little or as much as they want, but this exercise could keep a group busy for an hour or more. Put a time limit on it and continue the session.

Activity 14.3—Try new skills

PURPOSE: This activity promotes taking the risk to try new skills.

DESCRIPTION: Trying out new behavior involves risk—risk of failure. When you ask participants to teach each other, they may be nervous about demonstrating skills in front of their peers. You can reduce the anxiety by using teaching teams that allow participants to take the risks and feel supported by the team. This is true with reports, demonstrations, or performance in front of a group. Remind teams to encourage each other to take risks, and underscore the idea that taking risks leads to personal growth. You need only provide the opportunity; let adult participants decide to take the risk.

Activity 14.4—Share ideas

PURPOSE: Sharing ideas promotes risk taking.

DESCRIPTION: Everyone gains when people share ideas. The risk involved with exposing your ideas is in the fear that your idea may be criticized. Tell participants that once an idea is verbalized, it belongs to the group. That way any idea can be examined, modified, accepted, or rejected as needed without reflecting on the originator.

Adults like to share good ideas. Ask experienced providers to share their best child care program idea in a workshop, have a volunteer take good notes, and then arrange for the ideas to be typed and sent by mail or e-mail to each participant.

Activity 14.5—Perform before others

PURPOSE: Performing before others promotes risk taking and the thoughtful consideration of important information.

DESCRIPTION: One great thing about group learning that is superior to online learning or correspondence courses is that you have to perform before a group to some degree or another by sharing in a small group, reading a paper, making a group report, or demonstrating a skill. For example, after a group discussion, participants may be asked to report the results. Suggest that each group member take turns making the report, or use a team approach where each member makes a portion of a report. Making a report or sharing an idea with an audience of colleagues involves thoughtful consideration of important information and exercise of presentation skills, which promotes personal growth and greater learning.

Activity 14.6—Give-and-take debates

PURPOSE: Debates and discussions about disagreements promote risk taking and learning.

DESCRIPTION: Effective instructors welcome dialogue. We take a risk when we challenge another's ideas, because we also have to put forth our own ideas. One easy way to get a discussion going is to prepare some controversial statements that are sure to spark a debate. Read each statement and have participants move to one side of the room or the other based on their responses. Then hold a general discussion or have participants break into smaller groups for a dialogue between sides.

Activity 14.7—Instructor as model

PURPOSE: Instructor modeling promotes risk taking.

DESCRIPTION: Encourage taking risks whenever practical and possible by modeling risk-taking behavior. There are two ways an instructor can do that. First, share something about yourself and be willing to expose your shortcomings. Adults are more willing to risk change when the instructor is open and honest. Second, show an attitude of acceptance toward participants who make mistakes. This tells participants that the learning encounter is a safe place to take risks. For example, if a new child care applicant uses the term *babysitter* instead of *child care provider,* do not embarrass that person by openly correcting her. Jot down the error and teach proper terminology when it can be shared more impersonally.

Spontaneous Strategy 15—Take time to reflect

Arrange a time for silence, quiet reflection, or journaling to integrate new ideas. At certain times, restrict distractions and let the participants become inwardly spontaneous. It is often in the stillness of one's mind that deep and true change occurs. Be reluctant to fill every blank moment with words or activity.

Do not be afraid of silence in the classroom. It is not necessarily dead time. Dead time is when we are doing one thing and wish we could escape and do another thing. Time spent in silence alone or with others can be some of the most productive learning time, when thoughts are evoked and our cauldron of ideas is stirred.

If you have a choice of places to teach, find a room with natural lighting and clear windows. The room should not have piped-in elevator music or other white noise, such as loud heating or cooling units. The room should have movable chairs and a soft carpet for those who like to sit on the floor. The walls should not have unsightly or tasteless art. Muted colors with a few well-placed pieces of fine-art hangings would be great, but remember you need wall space for hanging theme posters, flip chart sheets, or participant displays.

The following activities will help you and participants take time to reflect.

Activity 15.1—Take breaks

PURPOSE: Breaks help participants reflect.

DESCRIPTION: Participants welcome breaks that allow them to think, talk, and react to what went on in the session. Scheduled breaks are good, but you can also take short breaks or stretch breaks. You can ask participants to call "break!" when they feel the need for a brief time out. If you have participants moving and working in small groups, tell them to take a personal break whenever they feel like it. Think of breaks as integral to your teaching.

If you want to know whether the group is ready for a break, ask, "Are there any questions?" If not, it is time for a break.

Activity 15.2—Journaling

PURPOSE: Journaling promotes reflection through writing.

DESCRIPTION: When you use journal writing in workshops, make a clear distinction between "note taking" and "journaling." Note taking is recording the workshop content, whereas journaling records the inner thoughts and feelings of participants in response to the learning experience. You can offer participants a special book or pad to use just for journaling rather than note taking.

Activity 15.3—Time between sessions

PURPOSE: Time between sessions allows reflection.

DESCRIPTION: Give an assignment to participants to spend time in silence. You can even teach a deep-breathing exercise for quieting and centering. (Two exercises similar to those taught in yoga are described in the following activities.) If you have more than one session over a period of days, consider assigning a portion of the time away from class for participants to quietly reflect on what they are learning.

Activity 15.4—Meditation

PURPOSE: Meditation promotes reflection.

DESCRIPTION: Meditation can be taught as a four-step process: relax, release, receive, and respond.

- Relax. Get comfortable; take deep breaths.
- Release. Let go of all extraneous thoughts and worries.
- Receive. Open your mind to all you are learning; seek insights and ways to apply it in your life and work.
- Respond. Tell others about your insights, or write in your journal about them.

Activity 15.5—Breathing

PURPOSE: Deep breathing promotes reflection.

DESCRIPTION: Here is a way to use breathing to promote reflection. Good breathing helps participants to relax, focus, and concentrate. These are important elements in listening and organizing thought, which in turn aids learning. First, simply become aware of your breathing (usually it is shallow chest breathing). Second, sit comfortably, relax, and exhale completely. Third, breathe in by pushing out your stomach and filling your abdomen with air and then your chest; count slowly to ten while doing this. Fourth, hold your breath to the count of five and then release your breath slowly to the count of ten. Repeat the sequence four or five times. This slow, rhythmic breathing soothes, calms, and reduces anxiety.

Activity 15.6—Thought stimulators

PURPOSE: Thought stimulators promote reflection.

DESCRIPTION: Provide thought stimulators such as questions, lecturettes, readings, or even a single word to start a reflection time. In an orientation for new child care applicants, the trainers ask them to reflect on what is unique about the care they will offer to children. After a few minutes of reflection, participants are asked to record their thoughts. At first they are taken aback by the question, because adults are not used to considering their unique talents. After some silence, however, pencils begin to move, and when it is time to share, many are surprised by what they discover about themselves and their uniqueness. A simple, well-timed question can open a participant's mind to brand-new worlds of thought, feeling, and learning.

Summary

Adult participants appreciate it when learning includes fun, surprise, and the element of risk. Participants also need times for reflection, when they can collect their thoughts and use their imaginations. Enjoyable and spontaneous learning creates an atmosphere of freedom and creativity. These aspects of instruction are evident when you use the learning activities from the Spontaneous Instructor Style. In the next chapter you will learn some ways to help participants feel safe and comfortable so they become more open to new learning.

The Safe Instructor Style: Strategies and learning activities

Adults need a comfortable, trust-filled learning environment in order to let go of the old and embrace the new. When adults feel accepted and know that their comfort zones are respected, they are able to drop their guard and relax. When they are certain that they won't be judged, participants will be more comfortable making the mistakes that are necessary for them to grow. The safe strategies and learning activities in this chapter will help you design instruction so participants trust you, each other, and your instruction.

Safe strategies include the following:
- Strategy 16—Help participants feel at home
- Strategy 17—Let participants know what to expect
- Strategy 18—Help participants get acquainted
- Strategy 19—Keep time commitments
- Strategy 20—Build trust and openness

Safe Strategy 16—Help participants feel at home

The learning space should help participants feel relaxed and welcome. Pay attention to creature comforts such as seating arrangements, refreshments, comfortable temperature and lighting, and rest rooms. Welcome participants with visual images that reflect the theme of the class. You may be forced to use facilities with less than desirable conditions, but try to make them comfortable. Design spaces for ease of interaction among adults. Also give some thought to pleasing all the senses: sight, hearing, smell, touch, and taste.

Pay attention to what the physical space communicates to your adult participants. Does it welcome them, or does it feel forbidding? A learning environment should communicate these seven assurances:

- You are welcome.
- You are important.
- You will be comfortable.
- You will enjoy yourself.
- You will learn.
- You will make friends.
- You will be safe.

The following activities help participants feel at home.

Activity 16.1: Early planning

PURPOSE: Early planning helps prevent problems.

DESCRIPTION: Sometimes you cannot predict what you might find when you arrive to teach at an unfamiliar site. Arrive early to scrutinize the site and make adjustments. Work with hosting services or make changes personally to ensure maximum comfort. Do not be afraid to rearrange things (but ask those in charge if you feel it is necessary). Keep in mind the kind of atmosphere you want. Consider displays, audiovisual equipment, where the "front" of the room should be for flip charts, and traffic flow to avoid being in the path of people entering or exiting the room. Pay attention to lighting, glare from the sun, and electrical-outlet placement. The more prepared you are, the more effective you will be. When you are in a pinch for time, involve early-arriving participants to help you set up. Be alert to special needs such as language interpreters and wheelchair accessibility. Avoid facilities for workshops where wheelchair accessibility is through a back door or through utility areas.

Activity 16.2: Personal greeting

PURPOSE: Personally greeting participants provides friendly human contact as participants enter.

DESCRIPTION: When leading a workshop, set up early so you can greet participants as they arrive. You want adult participants to feel at home and welcome. Volunteers or early-arriving participants can also fulfill this role. Participants may have questions or concerns that can be resolved before the class begins. As you greet participants, use that time to find out why they came so you can make the experience as meaningful to them as possible.

Even if you teach an ongoing class, it is still a good idea to arrive early, greet participants, and get to know them better.

Activity 16.3: Welcoming environment

PURPOSE: A welcoming environment makes learning inviting.

DESCRIPTION: Think about what welcomes you into a learning space. Attractive and informative posters, the smell of freshly brewed coffee and tea, and tasty snacks are a few things that give a friendly welcome. The room should be prepared with tables and chairs arranged for instruction. You may teach in some pretty nice and some pretty awful settings, but the important thing is to show participants that you have taken the time to prepare in order to provide a good learning experience.

Adult participants really enjoy soothing or upbeat music as they arrive in a workshop or class. Music is inviting and begins to build a sense of community as we all hear the music and feel the beat. Be sensitive to your group and try to choose music that most everyone enjoys—avoid extremes.

Activity 16.4: Displays

PURPOSE: Displays offer a center of interest.

DESCRIPTION: Display books and material that are related to your topic to offer participants an invitation to explore further. Create a center of interest with photographs, automatic slide shows, or other objects of interest to entice and enthrall your adult participants. If you teach child care workers, put out a display of your favorite toys to encourage free play. A display also provides a way to immediately engage participants in learning and offers relief to those who are not so gregarious.

Activity 16.5: Seating

PURPOSE: Use the seating arrangement to welcome participants.

DESCRIPTION: One good way to welcome participants is to have them enter a room already set up for small groups. Create table groupings for three to five participants. If the group is large, start with rows of chairs but then quickly move participants into groups. Movable chairs are best for this, but you may have to disconnect interlocking chairs—the time and energy is worth it.

Classrooms full of desks are a challenge, but they are relatively movable and can be rearranged into small groups.

Activity 16.6: Add your special touch

PURPOSE: Participants welcome special touches from the instructor.

DESCRIPTION: You may want to adorn your classroom in ways unique to you. Some instructors put toys or candies on each table for participants. Put culturally diverse posters on the walls or add patterned cloth on tables to provide a festive touch. You can also transform poor surroundings with flowers. Unique touches might reflect your particular instruction style or the content of the learning experience.

Safe Strategy 17—Let participants know what to expect

Provide participants with clear information about the training event: the objectives, requirements, agenda, dates and schedule, place, instructors, format, and cost. Solicit the participants' ideas and develop a workable match between planned activities and participants' needs and desires. Encourage participants to discuss and negotiate various aspects of the program to arrive at a workable arrangement.

One example of arriving at a workable arrangement occurred in a training session that got off to a late start. The published agenda did not match reality. The instructor, with some humor, held up the agenda sheet and declared it no longer valid. The class proceeded with a new plan, which eliminated any undue anxiety over the discrepancy. Everyone appreciated her candor and humor. If you find you have to wait for late-arriving participants, just declare a break for those present. This relieves tension and lets everyone know you want to include all involved, but that you are also aware of the timetable.

Developing a partnership between instructor and participant is an important aspect of working with adults. A partnership can take place when each side knows what to expect from the other. That is not to say that surprises or spontaneous twists and turns cannot take place, but avoid being needlessly sidetracked in ways that will waste time and energy. The following are guidelines and practices to develop this partnership in learning.

Listen to participants. Gather as much information as possible and feasible in order to understand what their expectations are. You may have little time to do this if the workshop is short, but you can spend a few minutes getting feedback from participants about what they wish to learn. If you have time and can contact some participants ahead of time, use a focus group to gather information. If you are teaching a workshop with multiple sessions, find out what participants expect in the first session and periodically check to find out if the content is meeting their expectations. Anonymity may be needed to get honest responses. You can use a "name optional" survey or request that participants meet together without you and write a summary of reactions.

Be honest and realistic about what you are offering to participants. Too often, particularly in short courses and workshops, little information is provided that tells participants what is going to happen. Titles and descriptions of these classes often do not fully explain the agenda. To reduce anxiety and confusion—an important part of the Safe Instructor Style—provide a detailed description of content as well as a complete agenda. Explain the plan clearly, and if change is needed be honest about it.

Come to an agreement. Bring the agenda discussion to a close by coming to an agreement. Usually just getting a nod of affirmation by the group is enough. "So we have agreed to have a break every hour on the hour, right?" In situations that are more complex, a written agreement may be necessary, such as on a flip chart sheet or on an overhead projector. It is essential to publicly acknowledge what decisions have been reached and seal the understanding with some symbol of agreement. Of course, you must keep the agreement.

The following activities help let participants know what to expect.

Activity 17.1: Share basic instructional information

PURPOSE: Sharing provides participants with basic instructional information.
DESCRIPTION: Here is a list of important information you should share with participants before getting started:

    course objectives
    basic course content
    course requirements

agenda or schedule

methods of instruction

fees

registration information

background and qualifications of the instructor

requirements to complete the class

Activity 17.2: Housekeeping

PURPOSE: Give out information about the space and procedures.

DESCRIPTION: Here are some things to let participants know about that will enhance their comfort and well-being:

rest room and telephone locations

snacks

breaks

meals

site rules—off-limit areas, equipment use, and so on

special-needs access

displays/resources

smoking policy

local opportunities—walks, trails, shopping, and so on

special events

breakout rooms

name tags

Activity 17.3: Special needs

PURPOSE: This activity informs participants of arrangements for meeting special needs.

DESCRIPTION: Will there be a need for a language or sign language interpreter? Will there be physical barriers that must be explained? What about literacy demands? Will participants be asked to read aloud or read instructions that may pose problems? Gain as much information as you can about what is required by participants with special needs, and try to find resources to meet these needs. If possible, inform people with special needs in advance if you cannot provide what they need.

Activity 17.4: Diversity

PURPOSE: This activity demonstrates appreciation of diversity among participants.

DESCRIPTION: Your advance publicity should include assurance that you are sensitive to and appreciate the diversity of your participants. Your instruction and instructional materials should present a nonbiased viewpoint with respect to culture and beliefs. Assure participants that your class does not discriminate based on ethnicity, culture, gender, or sexual orientation. You must also make reasonable accommodation for disabilities.

Activity 17.5: What to bring

PURPOSE: Let participants know what they need to provide.

DESCRIPTION: The list of items to bring may not be as long as the one you got when you went to summer camp, but participants should be told what they are expected to bring. A pen or pencil seems obvious, but you may need to mention other things. These might include a previously sent survey, resource lists to share, or special written assignments. If you know that the air conditioner is too cold, remind participants to bring a sweater, or to bring walking shoes if there is a wooded path nearby for a lunchtime stroll. Will you want sample child care records for study? Do you want participants to bring recyclable products to use as crafts? Help participants come prepared for any activity you plan so that no one will feel left out.

Activity 17.6: Changes

PURPOSE: This activity encourages instructors to inform participants of changes as soon as possible.

DESCRIPTION: It is disconcerting and disruptive when changes are made and participants are not informed. You do not want participants arriving at an empty room with no sign to guide them to the new room. If you plan changes in your curriculum or agenda, inform participants about it. If you have added a speaker who is not listed on the agenda, make special mention of this at the start of the workshop. When participants know what to expect, tension about changes often dissipates.

Activity 17.7: Be flexible

PURPOSE: This activity encourages flexibility in meeting expectations.

DESCRIPTION: Can you adjust your plan? If not, you may not want to teach adults. Sometimes, however, there may be time constraints, an inability to meet specific requests, or other limits placed on the instructor or the program. Facilitate compromises as needed. Again, be clear and provide information as early as possible. When there is a conflict, involve the participants in solving it—and make sure everyone understands the plan.

Safe Strategy 18—Help participants get acquainted

Plan get-acquainted exercises so participants can become familiar with each other, the topic, and the instructor. Devise a way to get adults actively involved with each other early on, but show sensitivity to participants' comfort zones. The best use of time is to combine topic-related activities with interpersonal connections. You are trying to build a sense of trust between adults and raise interest in the program.

Get-acquainted exercises are often left off the agenda because they are seen as frivolous and extraneous to learning. Quite the contrary! We are social beings and influenced by others, so introduction activities are central to learning.

You must gauge your activities to your participants, however. You want them to feel comfortable and not anxious, so select your warm-up activities carefully to help build bridges with your audience. If you know why getting-acquainted exercises are so important, and you approach them with confidence, you will find little resistance to them from adult participants.

People like to tell stories and talk about themselves. When participants reveal aspects of their lives, acceptance and appreciation shown by the group help individuals feel less threatened. Avoid the large-group "go around" introductions so commonly used. Such exercises usually just end up raising participants' anxiety. They do not listen to others because they are too busy preparing for or recovering from their own presentation. In most cases it is not necessary that everyone get to know about everybody else.

Small-group get-acquainted exercises help open possibilities for friendship, build rapport and cooperation, transform and heal the human spirit, break down barriers, and stimulate creativity. Here are some principles that guide get-acquainted and warm-up exercises:

- About 25 percent of the session time should be devoted to helping people get ready to learn.
- Give participants complete freedom to "pass" on any activity if they would rather not participate.
- Explain to participants what you are doing and why you are doing it. Seek general agreement before proceeding.
- Choose get-acquainted exercises with a clear purpose based on the learning task. The purposes of get-acquainted exercises include encouraging self-disclosure, building effective work teams, enhancing creativity, helping strangers feel at ease, and helping teams get closer as they face tough decisions. If it is feasible, the instructor should join the group in get-acquainted exercises.
- Use get-acquainted exercises that also introduce the topic of the session.

The following activities help participants get to know one another.

Activity 18.1: Tell your life story in one minute

PURPOSE: This activity promotes getting acquainted quickly.

DESCRIPTION: Form groups of two to four people. While the facilitator keeps time, ask participants to take turns telling their life stories in one minute. After all have shared, let groups explore any interesting bits of information gleaned from the exchange.

Activity 18.2: I imagine you . . .

PURPOSE: This helps participants who are somewhat acquainted to learn more about others in the group.

DESCRIPTION: Form groups of two to four people. Ask participants to choose partners and tell them what participants imagine their partners were like in sixth grade, junior high, and so on. Or ask them to imagine what the other's desk, garage, or hall closet looks like. Then ask participants to reveal the real description of themselves and compare that with the imagined one.

Activity 18.3: I want to know . . .

PURPOSE: This activity lets participants decide what they want to know about others.

DESCRIPTION: Group size can vary. Start by having each person write down several questions they want to know about others in the group. Let the group mill around. When you give a signal, have them stop and face the nearest person. Each person then asks the other a question from the list and gets a response. Signal the group to start milling around again. Repeat the process as often as you like. Instead of questions, you can ask participants to share something about themselves—job, three wishes, what would you do with a million dollars, and so on.

Activity 18.4: License plate

PURPOSE: This activity catches the essence of a person quickly.

DESCRIPTION: Form groups of four to six people. Have participants imagine they are creating a license plate (only seven letters or numbers may be used) that expresses their personality or a prominent aspect of their lives. Ask participants to write down their license plates and share them with the group. Then discuss, ask questions, and so on.

Activity 18.5: "Role" call

PURPOSE: To help the instructor and the other participants learn why people have come to the class.

DESCRIPTION: Use this with groups of up to thirty. (Add facilitators if the group is larger than thirty.) Have a flip chart, overhead, or whiteboard ready. As people enter the room for the first time, ask them what they do that brings them to this gathering. Make a list of each role on the flip chart and add slash marks for repeat answers. Encourage participants to talk with each other as the group gradually grows. When all have gathered, review the results of the "role" call.

VARIATION: Instead of roles, find out other interesting facts about participants.

Activity 18.6: I wish . . .

PURPOSE: To solicit expectations from the group.

DESCRIPTION: Form groups of two to five people. Have the groups answer these two questions: What do you wish would happen in this session? and What do you wish would not happen in this session? The groups report, and the instructor helps them clarify each point if necessary. Contract with the group to meet agreed-on expectations.

More get-acquainted exercises are described in Some More Ways to Get Acquainted (Table 5-1).

Safe Strategy 19—Keep time commitments

Instructors should stick to the schedule as agreed, or renegotiate it. Balance the schedule equally between the need to cover the material and the needs of participants. Provide information that helps participants understand what is at stake when changes are made.

There is nothing more irritating and distracting than to be in a meeting or training session and realize that the leader has lost track of the time. Adults fidget, look at watches, and generally suffer in silence. More information gets through when timelines are adhered to.

The following activities will help you manage presentation time effectively.

Activity 19.1: Budget your time

PURPOSE: Budgeting time promotes good planning.

DESCRIPTION: Rehearse every part of a workshop or class to get a general idea of how much time the various components or activities will take. If it looks as if you are squeezed for time (the most common problem), modify or eliminate sections. Rehearse presentations to get them well timed. Then write out a schedule listing your targeted times. If you wander or lose track of time, appoint a timekeeper to keep things flowing. Remember to publish an agenda and keep to that schedule.

TABLE 5-1

Some More Ways to Get Acquainted

You Are Unique

PURPOSE: Participants have fun sharing weird talents with each other.

DESCRIPTION: Group size can vary.

What little-known talent do you have? Let each person think about that and then show others what they can do: double whistle, cross eyes, walk on their hands, demonstrate their double-jointedness, and so on.

VARIATION: Reveal something that no one knows about you.

What's On Your Plate?

PURPOSE: This gets adults sharing about life and work.

DESCRIPTION: Form small groups up to five or six.

Ask participants to take turns telling what is on their plate in their lives or work, i.e., what is going on that is pleasing or concerning you in your life and work?

Things in Common, Things That Are Different

PURPOSE: This activity explores similarities and differences.

DESCRIPTION: Form small groups of two to ten.

The group begins listing things they have in common that are not very common. Ignore things like we all have two eyes, we all breathe, and so on. Go for the uncommon, such as we all were born east of the Rockies, we all adore cats, and so on. Share your list with the larger group. Go on to list the things that make each different from the others—what no one has in common.

No Social Props

PURPOSE: This allows more in-depth introductions.

DESCRIPTION: Start in pairs.

People introduce themselves without mentioning any roles they fill (you can't use job titles or parent roles), where they live or work, hobbies, or interests. Each pair joins with another pair. Each person introduces his or her partner to the new pair.

Who's Here Cheer

PURPOSE: This gives public acknowledgement of who is in the group.

DESCRIPTION: No limit to group size.

Have a set of variables ready (type of job, employer, values, life experience, and so on). As you name them, participants can stand and cheer if they fall into any of the categories. The louder cheer indicates the size or enthusiasm of those in the category.

Activity 19.2: Begin and end on time

PURPOSE: Keep time commitments for beginning and ending.

DESCRIPTION: Instructors need to be early! Prepare ahead of time so you can begin on time. Reward the people who come on time by taking time to answer some of their immediate questions while you wait for others. Adults are most perturbed when classes end late. In fact, they want to get out early, so design your session with that as a goal. If participants are checking their watches anxiously, your instruction may be for naught.

Activity 19.3: Transition time

PURPOSE: This activity allows for participant "nesting" needs.

DESCRIPTION: When participants have to travel far or rush between sessions, it helps to have a little time for transition. This is a basic need that can be thought of as human nesting time. We all need to settle down and get personally oriented from one situation to another. Casual conversation, networking with others, or eating snacks fulfills this need.

Activity 19.4: Keep control kindly

PURPOSE: This activity keeps the agenda and time on track by using gentle reminders.

DESCRIPTION: Let guest speakers know how much time they have to speak. Do not leave time allotments vague. Stand where participants will not see you so that you can, if necessary, signal the speaker with the "time" sign. With verbose participants, simply and kindly say, "Thanks, but we need to move on," and do so with resolve. If you are kind and firm in keeping control, everyone will be happy.

Activity 19.5: Publish the agenda

PURPOSE: A written agenda informs participants of timelines.

DESCRIPTION: The way to prevent problems is to always remember to publish an agenda for participants. No matter how informal the gathering or how short the session, always have an agenda. Participants need to know what will happen and what to expect. The agenda need not be very detailed, but there should be at least general topics and times given. You can convey the agenda by writing it on a flip chart, on a whiteboard, or in a simple handout.

Activity 19.6: Breaks

PURPOSE: Participants and instructors need breaks.

DESCRIPTION: Breaks are sacred. If you have published them as part of your plan, take them unless you have renegotiated break time with participants at the start of the workshop. Breaks can be scheduled or left up to the group whenever there is a need. Breaks and lunch, with participant agreement, may be used as part of class time, such as during small-group or partner discussions.

Activity 19.7: Getting back on track

PURPOSE: This activity allows flexibility while keeping the session on track.

DESCRIPTION: Sometimes it is advantageous to wander from the agenda in the interest of following a thread that is vital to the learning experience. Sometimes the wandering is the result of an instructor's losing control or working with a strong-willed and passionate group of participants. Below are some suggestions for getting back on track:

- Ask participants to be alert to when things get off track, and to say so.
- Clearly state the discrepancy between the plan and the current situation and be clear about the instructional consequences.
- Pay attention to the participants who seem uncomfortable with the diversion, and ask for their opinion.
- Most child care professionals are familiar with the concept of redirection in behavior management. That skill, with an adult spin, might be used profitably in such situations.

Safe Strategy 20—Build trust and openness

Participants get close when they discuss their important concerns and help each other solve problems. Employ group-building methods that encourage openness and problem solving. Use small groups, when practical, to provide a catalyst for the free flow of ideas. Closeness and trust help people take risks without fear of judgment. Strike a balance between intimacy and respect for comfort zones.

In a "Being a Better Listener" class, participants work in triads (groups of three). One of them listens, one observes, and one speaks. They take turns in each role. After an explanation about maintaining confidentiality, the participants are encouraged to talk about real problems in their lives. People have walked away amazed that they were able to be so candid with strangers and often find that they have received valuable help in the exchange. Trust takes time, so it is best to keep small groups together over an extended period of time.

Learning has been a breeding ground for many negative feelings. Fear and anxiety and even anger can be triggered by a learning task. Will I measure up? Will I be judged unfairly by the teacher? Will I be put on the spot? Will I be embarrassed or humiliated? Performance anxiety is almost universal in our competitive society. We build it into everything.

You might think adults would feel self-assured and confident in learning new things, since they have been learning all their lives. For most of us, our learning experiences have been in schools and colleges—formal educational settings. In that environment, learning was demanded, not encouraged. Grades represented an external reward or punishment for a level of performance. Expectations from teachers, peers, and parents, combined with the demands we put on ourselves, often created pressures and conflicts. Instructors can do much to minimize performance anxiety by using strategies that reassure adult learners.

The following activities help to build trust among participants.

Activity 20.1: Stress confidentiality

PURPOSE: To help participants keep confidentiality when needed.

DESCRIPTION: Some classroom discussions go better when you stress the need to treat as confidential anything heard within the course of the learning experience. This is one of the items listed in Safe Rules for Learning Together (Table 5-2). Confidentiality encourages honest sharing, and when it is stressed, adults are most willing to comply.

TABLE 5-2

Safe Rules for Learning Together

Be a good active listener.

Judge ideas, not people.

You are free to pass.

Encourage each other to take risks.

Keep personal confidences.

Activity 20.2: Your attitude counts

PURPOSE: To communicate enthusiasm for learning.

DESCRIPTION: Do you enjoy learning? Are you looking forward to this experience? Your excitement about the learning experience will help your participants catch the mood. Know and believe in what you are about to teach. Do you have a clear picture of your goal? Have you prepared learning activities that will accomplish the goal? Do you believe the learning experience will benefit the participants? Your belief in your goal and approach will translate into a confident demeanor that will put your participants at ease—even if inwardly you are a little nervous. By the way, do not be afraid to say you are nervous. It will serve to show you can be trusted for your honesty.

Activity 20.3: Be a good listener

PURPOSE: To promote listening among participants.

DESCRIPTION: When we are listened to, we trust. The instructor needs to model good listening skills and teach participants to listen carefully to each other. A good listening guideline for adults is to tell them they are free to make side comments to one another while you talk, but to listen very closely to their fellow participants. Once this guideline is presented, the instructor can feel free to remind participants to listen carefully.

Activity 20.4: Small-group sharing

PURPOSE: To use small-group sharing to build trust.

DESCRIPTION: Small groups simulate the family, which may be why they are such a powerful force in learning and promoting personal growth. The use of triads is an excellent instruction tool. (See The Triad Ten, Table 5-3.) Remember that keeping groups together over time promotes greater trust.

TABLE 5-3

The Triad Ten

Ten Reasons for Using Groups of Three in Teaching Adults

Intimacy: The group is small enough to provide intimacy and personal disclosure.

Discussion: The group is large enough to get lively discussion with multiple points of view.

Fairness: Each member can contribute with less chance for domination by any member.

Bonding: The small group helps promote cohesion among members. It simulates a family.

Combinations: The triad can be combined easily with other triads to form larger groups for other purposes.

Learning roles: Three roles can be assigned: observer-recorder, listener-receiver, speaker-actor.

Safety: The group is "safe." Embarrassment is at a minimum for exercises like role-playing and strategy practice.

Flexibility: The group works well in large or small training workshops. In large groups, the triad promotes intimacy. In smaller groups, it allows using intergroup dynamics (for example, two triads can exchange).

Cooperation: The odd number (three) helps avoid stalemates in decision making.

Mobility and scheduling: A group of three can easily move for training exercises, and three group members can coordinate personal schedules for out-of-session assignments.

Activity 20.5: Working and playing together

PURPOSE: To build trust through mutual activities.

DESCRIPTION: A powerful bond develops when people accomplish things or recreate together. Plan to involve groups in problem solving, working, and playing together. For example, ask child care providers to play together in games or other activities they typically organize for their children. When groups support their members in these activities, they will reach their goals successfully and experience a satisfying, energizing, and motivating way to learn and grow.

Activity 20.6: Respect what they know

PURPOSE: This builds trust.

DESCRIPTION: A maxim: Do not insult the participants' intelligence. Acknowledge the range of knowledge and skill in a group. At the beginning of a class or workshop, make an effort to know the group by assessing their experience and knowledge—use an exercise such as activity 18.5, "Role" Call. Design your class so that more advanced participants gain recognition and perhaps take the role of mentor to others. Also, you might consider referring to your lecturettes as information for some and a review for others. Most adults appreciate a review of previously learned knowledge.

Activity 20.7: Model openness and trust

PURPOSE: This reminds instructors to set the tone for openness.

DESCRIPTION: Probably the most potent way to influence trust and openness in participants is to model it. Let participants know you are human, and be honest about your incomplete understanding of your topic. Acknowledge your own struggles to grow in understanding, knowledge, and skill. Share personal information and opinions to some degree, so that participants can identify with you.

At the same time, trust your participants to want to know and grow. Trust them in their work groups to be diligent and responsible, and realize that they are works in progress just as you are. Teaching is not about hero worship. Teaching is a relationship that aims for greater understanding, knowledge, and skill.

Summary

Adult participants want to feel comfortable and be at ease in a learning environment. Feeling safe is a prerequisite for a positive learning experience. By using the learning activities from the Safe Instructor Style you will ensure that adults feel at home and are prepared to learn.

These last four chapters have presented many strategies and learning activities that can be used to encourage learning through systematic, stimulating, spontaneous, and safe instruction. These four instructor styles must be balanced to set the stage for adult learning. In chapter 6, you will learn how to design learning so that the four styles are balanced.

Planning for balanced instruction

In previous chapters, we made a distinction between *style, strategy,* and *activity.* In this chapter, you will learn how to plan using *strategies* drawn from the four instructor *styles.* The sample workshop in this chapter will show you how to blend the strategies to create a teaching plan that reflects a balanced teaching style. Chapter 7 will show you how to implement a teaching plan using a blend of *strategies* and *activities* from each of the four instructor styles.

Balance is best

To properly employ the four instructor styles and ensure the best learning experience for your participants, you must make sure the styles operate in balance. Participants should benefit equally from each style. They will know the logic of your instruction (systematic), they will be challenged to learn (stimulating), they will experience surprise and humor (spontaneous), and they will feel comfort and trust while learning (safe).

Balance is difficult to achieve if an instructor is not flexible. The two main errors made by instructors are that they teach the way they learn, or they teach the way they were taught. As instructors, we can become rigid in our style and our use of strategies, especially when we try to maintain our own personal comfort. One instructor may want a logical plan at the expense of more spontaneity. Another instructor may not take enough time to help people feel safe and comfortable because he wants to jump right into presenting his ideas. A third instructor may spend too much time and energy with group fun and games and largely ignore the use of logic in planning.

As you study the strategies, begin to identify the ones you tend to avoid or use less often. Learning to appreciate and use all twenty strategies will help you find creative balance in instructor styles. Improvement comes with helpful and accurate assessment, critical reflection, and willingness to risk trying new ways. When you examine and broaden the way you teach, you will better serve the adults you teach. Those strategies you seldom employ will most likely be the ones you should use and improve. Most trainers, even beginners, have a natural talent for using some of the strategies. Mastering other strategies will require that you learn and practice them to improve your performance.

A planning sequence

A balance of the four instructor styles can be achieved through a sequence of steps. Use these steps to guide you through a natural progression of planning using each of the instructor styles and strategies. This chapter presents the steps in detail and uses a sample workshop to help you visualize how the strategies can be combined in planning to create a balanced teaching style.

The recommended planning sequence is as follows:

- **Step 1**—Plan using the Systematic Instructor Style and strategies. This step helps you establish the basic goals and outline for your instructional program.
- **Step 2**—Plan using the Stimulating Instructor Style and strategies. This step helps you design a program that will meet your instructional goals.
- **Step 3**—Plan using the Spontaneous Instructor Style and strategies. This step helps you make the instruction enjoyable and unique.
- **Step 4**—Plan using the Safe Instructor Style and strategies. This step helps you comfortably draw participants into the experience you have designed.

Instructor Planning Notes (Table 6-1) is a form you can use to record your ideas as you follow these steps. The following workshop demonstrates each of the four steps in detail.

TABLE 6-1

Instructor Planning Notes

Use this form to incorporate each instructor style into your sessions. It is best to follow the planning sequence as outlined below.

General topic: _____

Summary of the most important ideas to cover: _____
_____
_____

1. SYSTEMATIC = Well planned and cooperatively designed. How will I assess learning needs? How will I involve participants in the plan? What are possible goals and specific objectives? What is my tentative teaching plan? How will I evaluate?

2. STIMULATING = Active learning, new ideas, solves real problems. What new, provocative, or inspiring ideas will I teach? How can I make learning active? How can I help participants solve real problems in their daily lives?

3. SPONTANEOUS = Humor, fun, surprise, reflection. How will I get participants to interact freely? How will I encourage risk taking? How can I introduce fun, surprise, or humor? Should I plan for personal reflection or journal writing? If so, how?

4. SAFE = Comfortable learning space, closeness, and trust. How will I design the learning space for comfort? What types of warm-up activities and group building will I use? How will I ensure respect and consideration for participant needs?

A sample workshop

The sample workshop "What's My Style?" (WMS), designed for child care center managers and directors, will show the principle of balanced styles in action. A description of the WMS workshop is presented along with the planning sequence to illustrate each point.

This sample workshop was designed as a two-hour workshop within a larger child care conference. In this workshop you will recognize some of the same concepts used in *Teach with Style*, which are adapted to teach managers how to gain balance in administering and supervising child care center staff and programs. The learning goals of the WMS workshop are for child care center directors to know how to balance their management style and to know the characteristics of a learning organization. The workshop also presents a process for job-skills coaching that helps managers improve their ability to influence organizational development.

This chapter ends with an outline of the "What's My Style?" workshop and some sample handouts.

Step 1—Plan using the Systematic Instructor Style and strategies

In this step you will decide how you will involve participants in the planning. How will you assess the needs of participants? What are the specific goals or objectives on which you will focus? What are the main content points and methods you will use? How will you evaluate the effectiveness of your instruction? Refer to chapters 2, 3, 4, and 5 for detailed descriptions of strategies and learning activities for each of the four instructor styles. Begin your planning with these strategies to guide you.

The strategies that will help you incorporate the Systematic Instructor Style include the following:

- Strategy 1—Collaborate with participants as you plan
- Strategy 2—Assess participant learning needs and styles
- Strategy 3—Set clear, meaningful goals
- Strategy 4—Plan to reach your goals
- Strategy 5—Evaluate your plan

Strategy 1—Collaborate with participants as you plan. It is best when an instructor can meet directly with participants or their representatives and involve them in planning the instruction. If that is not possible, do whatever you can to get information about the needs, characteristics, and desires of those you will teach.

WMS: *The instructor met with a group of child care center directors who affirmed that the concepts to be taught in the workshop were relevant to their group. In fact, this group was able to provide important information, which resulted in some modifications in the design of the content and methods. Collaboration with the child care conference staff, who sponsored the workshop, also affirmed that the general content of WMS was important and should be added to the conference offerings. The class description was listed in the conference brochure, and the instructor was confident that it would draw participants who wanted and needed this kind of instruction.*

Strategy 2—Assess participant learning needs and styles. The instructor should attempt to get an accurate picture of the participants, including their needs, interests, learning styles, and challenges. In classes held over several sessions, there is ample opportunity to glean this information. Often, however, in short courses or workshops, the information may have to come directly from participants in the first few moments of the course. This new information may mean you have to modify your plans, so prepare with this in mind.

WMS: *The instructor had no chance to assess the needs of the participants prior to the workshop. Consequently, the instructor used three methods to get a quick assessment:*

1. *As participants arrived, the instructor greeted them and asked them what their job role was and what they hoped to gain from the workshop. This role and course content information was recorded on flip chart sheets for all twenty-four participants and reviewed early in the class.*

2. *The instructor listed the objectives and the agenda for the workshop and asked participants to indicate agreement or disagreement with them.*

3. *The instructor had the participants spend a few minutes in small groups discussing and reporting what they wished would and would not happen in the workshop. This was also recorded on flip chart sheets for all to see.*

Strategy 3—Set clear, meaningful goals. The instructor should establish the goals for instruction based on the needs, interests, and learning styles of the participants. The goals (or "objectives") are your blueprints for the instructional design.

WMS: *The objectives for the class were based initially on the feedback received from a prior meeting with the center directors and from conversations with the conference staff. The five objectives were listed on the cover of the workshop handout packet. The feedback from the needs assessment done in the first minutes of the workshop showed that these objectives were appropriate and well targeted for these participants. (See page 111 for a list of the WMS objectives.)*

Strategy 4—Plan to reach your goals. The instruction should be designed to reach the established goals. This is done by carefully planning curriculum based directly on the goals. In the initial stages of planning, the instructor designs the program with broad, general ideas. More specific content and methods can be put into place later.

WMS: *The instructor designed the program based on the five objectives. The instructor had to allow time to present the basic principles behind the management style and organizational model. Time was also set aside for the participants to assess their styles and to develop plans for improving both their management and their organizations. The instruction was designed so that the participants would enjoy the learning experience. The instructor had just two hours to present this program, so precise timing was worked out while providing for flexibility to change according to participant needs.*

Strategy 5—Evaluate your plan. Early in the planning stages the instructor should design a way to determine to what extent the program design meets the goals. The evaluation method you choose should match the situation: How precise does the information need to be? Who needs the information? What is the purpose of the evaluation? If the information is designed primarily to help the instructor improve, then you will want direct feedback on your impact as an instructor. If participants need to pass a standard exam in the future based on this instruction, you will want to assess the level of participant performance. Often in conferences and workshops you will simply want to ask participants whether the instruction met their goals.

WMS: *The conference staff had already designed a workshop evaluation. Given the two-hour time frame, it was impractical to ask participants to spend much time beyond filling out the conference-designed form. The conference staff wanted to know whether the instructor was effective as a trainer and whether the workshop was helpful to the participants for their purposes. If time had permitted, the instructor might have asked participants to rate the extent to which each objective was met.*

Step 2—Plan using the Stimulating Instructor Style and strategies

In this step the instructor decides specifically what the content will be and how it will be presented. What new and useful ideas will be presented? How will participants be engaged in active learning activities? How will you help participants solve real problems they will face? How will you encourage the creative powers of the participants to use new learning? And finally, how will you help participants practice new skills?

The strategies that will help you incorporate the Stimulating Instructor Style include:

- Strategy 6—Present information in interesting, useful ways
- Strategy 7—Use active learning approaches
- Strategy 8—Encourage creativity
- Strategy 9—Help participants solve real problems
- Strategy 10—Help participants practice new learning

Strategy 6—Present information in interesting, useful ways. Some learning involves review of material, but primarily instructors need to lead their participants into new territory and challenge them. Learning is most effective when the participant can put it to good use immediately.

WMS: *The content of the workshop was new to the participants. The material was presented through handouts, lecturettes, overheads, and inventories that the participants filled out. For the most part, participants were experienced center* *directors and supervisors, and as the material was being presented, they realized that it was relevant to helping them become more effective in their jobs. There was a direct connection of the content to their role as child care center managers.*

Strategy 7—Use active learning approaches. It is always a challenge to instructors to make learning active. As human beings, we tend to follow what seems to be the quickest and easiest way. As instructors that means using words to teach and dismissing the more difficult task of involving the participant actively at least 50 percent of the time.

WMS: *The instructor used several methods to make sure participants were involved actively in learning.*
- *In the first few moments of the workshop, participants were involved in small-group discussions.*
- *Participants were asked to fill out inventories and analyze them.*
- *Participants read and discussed material presented in handouts.*
- *Participants were asked to interview each other using a guide sheet.*
- *The participants worked together to solve management problems and plan for improvement.*
- *Participants asked questions, which were answered by other participants as well as the instructor. Only a few minutes were taken up by direct instruction.*

Strategy 8—Encourage creativity. A powerful tool for change and growth is blending learning and creative thought. The effects of your teaching are magnified when participants use the new material they are learning to generate ideas and solutions.

WMS: *The workshop involved having participants apply new models for management styles and organizational development to solving problems and making creative changes in their organizations. The instructor facilitated this process so that each participant became a client and a consultant. These roles allowed the participants to originate new ways of thinking, organizing, and acting. The structured process in the workshop left participants free to explore within the limits set.*

Strategy 9—Help participants solve real problems. New learning is valuable when it helps participants work on real problems in life and work. The instructor provides some time to help participants integrate the new learning with their real-world issues.

WMS: *The main focus of the WMS workshop was helping child care center directors become more effective in their jobs. The instructor made certain that real problems of the participants were the focus of the workshop. The participants filled out inventories pertaining to their roles as managers, worked on analyzing their organizations, and then applied this information in making real plans to solve real problems back home.*

Strategy 10—Help participants practice new learning. The optimal way to teach is to have participants actually apply what is learned in a real-world setting. This can be done through simulations or role plays to put skills, knowledge, and understanding to the test.

WMS: *The directors paired off and held simulated job-skills coaching interviews. They focused on improving their management style and organizational operation. The two-hour time frame put some limits on direct practice of the model, but the participants made personal and organizational development plans to put their new learning to use on the job. If there had been more time, the instructor would have arranged a simulated staff meeting for participants to rehearse some of the planned changes in their styles.*

Step 3: Plan using the Spontaneous Instructor Style and strategies

In this step the instructor reviews the curriculum to find room for some planned serendipity. How will you help participants share their stories? How will you make the experience enjoyable? How could you weave humor into the mix? Will you integrate times for reflection or journaling? How will you facilitate risk taking for the sake of learning?

The strategies that will help you incorporate the Spontaneous Instructor Style include the following:

- Strategy 11—Help participants tell their stories

- Strategy 12—Make it funny, make it fun
- Strategy 13—Use imagination and the arts
- Strategy 14—Build in risk taking
- Strategy 15—Take time to reflect

Strategy 11—Help participants tell their stories. Adults like to tell their stories, and this desire can be tapped for the benefit of learning. Make sure adults have a chance to talk intimately about your topic and their interests in and struggles with it.

WMS: *The participants began telling their stories right away when the instructor asked participants to share "what is on your plate" in a warm-up exercise. The participants wanted to talk with other administrators; this was a rare opportunity for them. The participants completed the two inventories, one on personal management style and one on learning organization. The participants talked in pairs about the need for change and plans for improvement. Ample opportunity for sharing stories was provided during the two-hour workshop.*

Strategy 12—Make it funny, make it fun. Participants are more open to learning and change when they laugh and enjoy themselves. What may appear to be silliness and unnecessary banter may in fact indicate that participants are able to relax and learn. Promote this sense of fun in your classes and workshops with adults.

WMS: *The instructor used humor right from the start. The workshop site was a formal lecture hall with rows of desk-seats steeply terraced down to the lecture podium. As participants entered from the top, the instructor seemed to be in a pit far below, so the instructor used humor to coax participants into the front rows.*

The instructor used the "I Wish . . . " activity (activity 18.6, described in chapter 5) to give participants an opportunity to say what they liked and disliked in workshops. The instructor brought out the humor in the situation by having participants focus on what they do not wish to happen (long, boring lectures; rehashing old stuff; and so on).

Throughout the workshop, the instructor used informal humor to talk about the topics. In addition, the participants laughed and enjoyed themselves as they shared their mutual foibles in managing child care centers, a topic that invariably involves humorous situations.

Strategy 13—Use imagination and the arts. Although music, art, and other forms of creative expression are seldom used to teach adults, many participants find it helpful. Whenever appropriate, use the talents and the imaginations of participants in your teaching. Learners benefit from the involvement of the whole person in the process.

WMS: *The instructor asked participants to imagine being back in their work roles. The instructor played soft, pleasant music to help them relax. Participants were asked to imagine how their workplaces would be if positive changes were in place. Given more time, the instructor could have used poetry, sculpture, or collages to help participants visualize changes in their workplaces. For example, participants could be asked to write a poem or song to illustrate how their organizations might look when transformed.*

Strategy 14—Build in risk taking. To learn, change, or grow takes risk. Instructors serve their participants well by facilitating risk taking. The risk is not necessarily great, but participants need to be given the opportunity to move from the known to the unknown, which will move participants toward positive change.

WMS: *The instructor presented opportunities for participants to take the risk of self-disclosure. If participants were able to be honest with themselves and others, they could better diagnose problems and accurately target needed changes in their managerial style and organizational development. Through the "What's on Your Plate?" exercise (see chapter 4, activity 14.2), self-disclosure telescoped into sharing the results of personal and organizational profiles.*

Strategy 15—Take time to reflect. Often, needed insight and change occur when we have an opportunity to reflect on new learning. Instructors should provide for this in their teaching. Resist the temptation to fill every moment with words and activities.

WMS: *This workshop provided times for participants to reflect after they had filled out the two inventories. After participants finished the analysis, they could think about its implications. Another option would have been to ask participants to begin the first few pages of a journal called "My Management Journal," to be used throughout the year as they apply new insights gained in the workshop.*

Step 4—Plan using the Safe Instructor Style and strategies

In this step the instructor decides how to use the learning space and the activities to help participants feel comfortable and ready to learn. How will you make participants feel at home in the learning environment? How will you tell or show participants what to expect? How will you help participants get acquainted with each other? How will you ensure that time commitments are made and met? How will you help participants to become trusting and open in your workshop?

The strategies that will help you incorporate the Safe Instructor Style include the following:

- Strategy 16—Help participants feel at home
- Strategy 17—Let participants know what to expect
- Strategy 18—Help participants get acquainted
- Strategy 19—Keep time commitments
- Strategy 20—Build trust and openness

Strategy 16—Help participants feel at home. The instructor needs to create a learning space that helps participants relax, feel comfortable, and settle into learning. The space should welcome participants and invite them to learn what you have to teach.

WMS: *As described earlier, this workshop was held in a lecture hall that seated more than a hundred participants in rigid, stationary desk-chairs. The rows of seats were terraced in a steep slant down toward a stage-like floor with a large podium stationed in front of a huge blackboard. Making twenty-five partici-pants feel comfortable was not easy. The instructor placed a compact disc player near the entrance and played pleasant, soothing background music. Signs were* *put up pointing the way to the workshop location, and a welcome sign was placed near the door. The instructor arranged an attractive display of topical books and materials in the front to draw participants in. An overhead projector (brought in by the instructor) projected an attractive image on a screen. The instructor warmly greeted each person, helped each one find a seat near the front, and started with brief, informal interviews using the "Role" Call activity (see chapter 5, activity 18.5). Each person's role and reasons for attending the workshop were listed on a flip chart and posted at the front of the room for all to see.*

Strategy 17—Let participants know what to expect. Make sure participants have a clear idea about what will happen. Give participants the essential information such as objectives of the class, an agenda or schedule of events, and what is expected of them.

WMS: *After providing some housekeeping details (location of rest rooms, timing of breaks, and so on) and an initial warm-up exercise, the instructor handed each person a packet of materials. The packet included the workshop objectives and agenda, relevant handouts, and participant inventories. The instructor reviewed all of these materials and allowed time for questions. The results of the "Role" Call exercise were discussed in light of the agenda. Next, the "I Wish . . ." exercise (chapter 5, activity 18.6) took place. Small groups of participants discussed and reported what they did and did not want to happen in the workshop. The instructor described which wishes could be honored and made some adjustments to accommodate these requests. In the end, the participants had a pretty good idea of what would happen, what they would gain from the experience, and what was expected of them.*

Strategy 18—Help participants get acquainted. Adults are freer to concentrate on the learning tasks when they feel socially safe. Getting acquainted with other participants is not frivolous; it is an essential aspect of adult learning. Participants who are acquainted and comfortable with others will be more committed and attentive.

WMS: *The instructor selected three methods for helping the WMS participants get acquainted.*

- *As participants entered, the instructor interviewed each one and posted their job roles and their reasons for attending the class. This provided a way for participants to see who was there and why.*
- *In small groups, participants shared in the "What's on Your Plate?" exercise (see Table 5-1). This allowed participants to disclose some things about themselves, relieve some stress, and identify with other participants—a great beginning for building groups.*
- *Participants shared their wishes about what they wanted to happen in the class through the "I Wish . . ." exercise. This helped participants feel a sense of control over the learning experience as well as start the process of group problem solving.*

At the end of these three experiences, the participants were happily talking, working, and laughing together—a good sign that the activities had worked.

Strategy 19—Keep time commitments. It is vital to keep a handle on time. Adult participants become agitated when they see time slipping out of control. Watch the time, control the time, or modify the time as needed.

WMS: *The instructor published the schedule in the workshop packet and on a flip chart. (A copy is printed at the end of this chapter.) The schedule was followed closely, and the break was taken as planned. In addition, the instructor assured participants that the class would end a few minutes early, and it did. Once dismissed, participants were free to talk with the instructor and look over the book display.*

Strategy 20—Build trust and openness. An important aspect of the Safe Instructor Style is making certain that participants feel a sense of trust and are open to learning. A good way to do this is through your own trustworthiness and through the use of activities, primarily small-group activities, that get participants working and talking together.

WMS: *This workshop relied heavily on small-group work and trust building. The get-acquainted exercises (see strategy 18 on the previous page) started the work of building trust, and then participants worked in the same* *groups to analyze inventories and work on management and organizational improvements. In fact, the main learning that took place in this workshop happened in small, intimate work groups where participants felt safe to reveal problems and solve them with others in the group. To strengthen this process, the instructor emphasized that the participants all face difficult assignments in the field of child care administration, so no one should feel shy in working together toward more effective administration and organizational functioning.*

"What's My Style?" workshop outline

The objectives and agenda below integrate all four styles and draw on multiple strategies to deliver an effective learning experience. An important aspect of the Safe Instructor Style is to make the learning objectives and agenda clear by publishing them.

Objectives:

Learn a manager-style model.

Identify your style as a manager.

Analyze your organization.

Plan for personal and organizational development.

Agenda:

Greetings by instructor and "Role" Call exercise

"What's on Your Plate?" exercise

Introduction and distribution of workshop packets

"I Wish . . ." exercise

What's My Style?

Lecturette 1: Balance of Styles

Small-group discussion

Lecturette 2: Balance in Learning Organizations

Small-group discussion

Lecturette 3: AIM in Job Skills Coaching

Job-skills coaching interviews

Wrap-up and evaluation

Summary

The "What's My Style?" workshop offers a real-life example of how to plan a teaching and learning experience using multiple strategies to create balanced instruction. The suggested sequence of steps can be used as a planning guide that will help you incorporate each of the instructor styles and strategies. Chapter 7 will show you how to implement a teaching plan using a blend of strategies and activities from each of the four instructor styles.

Practical application of the instructor styles, strategies, and learning activities: A workshop

The preceding chapters provide a general understanding of the Teach with Style model. This chapter offers a sample workshop designed for child care providers that demonstrates how to implement the model. It shows how the specific learning activities can be selected to provide an interesting and useful program for participants. Use your imagination as you read so you can place yourself in the roles of instructor and learner. Think about how you would feel and react to each activity. How would you make it better? How would you redesign it to fit your unique situation and personal strengths? How can you apply the same structure to other subjects you may want to teach? What other learning activities might you add to enhance the learning experience or to balance your heavier reliance on one or two instructor styles?

Sample workshop: "Managing Misbehavior in Children"

This workshop is designed for child care providers in any setting—home, center, and school-age programs. Managing misbehavior in children is something that most providers find challenging. This sample workshop offers caregivers a simple, logical approach to handling behavior problems in the child care setting. Instead of giving solutions, it teaches providers to use a process for discovering the causes of problems, setting goals, and finding solutions. This example demonstrates how to use specific learning activities, which are summarized in Tables 7-1 and 7-2.

TABLE 7-1

Workshop Agenda
"Managing Misbehavior in Children"

Topic	Objective	Activity/Content	Materials
Preparation	To inform and prepare participants to learn	Instructor sets up book display table; laptop computer with music and slide show; posters and overhead projector displaying images. Arranges chairs, sets up flip chart, and places a small snack on each chair.	Books, laptop, music, posters, tape, flip chart and markers, extra pencils, paper, overhead projector and transparencies, handouts, and snacks
Introduction (15 min.)	To build groups and prepare to learn	Instructor shows and tells about goals, agenda, and methods of learning. Announces necessary housekeeping items. Solicits comments and agreement on workshop plan. **Exercise:** Instructor divides participants into groups of three. Individuals in each group take turns telling their life stories in one minute.	Flip chart and markers, handout, or overhead
Define *misbehavior* (10 min.)	To define and focus on our topic	**Lecturette:** Instructor defines *misbehavior* and solicits the group's reaction. Redefines if needed.	Flip chart and markers, handout, or overhead with definition
Identify misbehavior (20 min.)	To identify child behaviors that may be troublesome	**Exercise:** Small groups of three write lists of problem behaviors as seen by child caregivers. Groups report; a volunteer writes behaviors on the flip chart, posts lists around room.	Papers, pencils, flip chart, and markers

Break (10 min.)

TABLE 7-1

Workshop Agenda, continued

Topic	Objective	Activity/Content	Materials
Explore and identify cause of misbehavior (20 min.)	To explore and identify possible causes of misbehavior in a child and build cohesive small groups	**Exercise:** Small groups discuss causes for misbehavior. Instructor lists categories of possible causes of behavior; participants see if any causes they listed fit the categories.	Flip chart and markers
Learn the AIM approach (30 min.)	To learn an approach to handling child misbehavior	**Lecturette:** Knowing the cause guides a provider's response. A = Actual behavior (List, define, and give examples for ways to assess behavior.) I = Ideal (Define and give examples for setting a goal.) M = Method (List, define, and give examples of ways to respond to misbehavior.)	Handout of AIM approach with room for taking notes
Break (10 min.)			
Reflection (5 min.)	To provide a time for thoughtful consideration	**Exercise:** Instructor asks participants to spend a few quiet minutes thinking about a child or situation they want to discuss.	
Peer consultation (40 min.)	To learn to use the AIM approach	**Exercise:** Individuals in small groups take turns discussing a situation, using AIM as outline.	Handout of AIM approach
Evaluation and wrap-up (10 min.)	To solicit reactions to the workshop and answer any questions	Instructor asks participants to fill out evaluation forms and solicits questions and comments from group about workshop.	Handout of evaluation form

TABLE 7-2

Summary of Instructor Styles, Strategies, and Activities in the "Managing Misbehavior in Children" Workshop

Module	Style	Strategy	Activity	
Introduction	Safe	19. Keep time commitments	19.5	
		17. Let participants know what to expect	17.1	17.2
	Systematic	1. Collaborate with participants as you plan	1.3	
		3. Set clear, meaningful goals	3.5	
Warm-up	Safe	18. Help participants get acquainted	18.1	
	Spontaneous	14. Build in risk taking	14.1	14.2
		11. Help participants tell their stories	11.1	11.3
Explore and identify misbehavior	Safe	17. Let participants know what to expect	17.7	
	Spontaneous	14. Build in risk taking	14.2	14.4
	Stimulating	7. Use active learning approaches	7.6	
Break	Spontaneous	15. Take time to reflect	15.1	
Explore and identify causes of misbehavior	Stimulating	7. Use active learning approaches	7.6	
		8. Encourage creativity	8.1	
		6. Present information in interesting, useful ways	6.1	6.3
	Safe	20. Build trust and openness	20.5	
Learn the AIM approach	Stimulating	6. Present information in interesting, useful ways	6.1	6.3
		10. Help participants practice new learning	10.6	
Break	Safe	19. Keep time commitments	19.6	
Reflection	Spontaneous	15. Take time to reflect	15.6	
Peer consultation	Stimulating	9. Help participants solve real problems	9.2	
	Spontaneous	11. Help participants tell their stories	11.1	11.2
	Stimulating	10. Help participants practice new learning	10.1	
Evaluation and wrap-up	Systematic	5. Evaluate your plan	See page 32.	

Plan for "Managing Misbehavior in Children"

This workshop topic is relevant to most child care providers and, as such, would typically be advertised using the title and a brief description. The participants will have only a minimal sense of the content, and the teacher will not know anything about participants until they show up at the specified time. This typical scenario offers little opportunity for collaboration between participants and the instructor before the session. If the instructor has contracted with a specific group of caregivers, a meeting can take place in advance to help the teacher get information about specific learning needs and a profile of participants using activity 1.1: A Learning Team Approach and activity 1.2: Representative Group (Systematic/Collaborate with Participants As You Plan; see chapter 2). The instructor can then design or modify the program based on these findings.

In many cases, the instructor has prepared a workshop topic in advance or has a particular slant on a topic that will be taught. In the case of the "Managing Misbehavior in Children" workshop, the instructor can use a number of strategies and activities to gather information from participants at the start of the workshop. Collaborative learning activities work well to achieve this goal, such as activity 1.3: On-the-Spot Collaboration or activity 1.6: Small-Group In-Session Collaboration (Systematic/Collaborate with Participants As You Plan; see chapter 2).

Though assessing learning styles for a short course like this may be difficult, the best approach is to use a variety of teaching methods that meet a broad range of needs. You can also make some assessments about participant learning styles when you observe participants as you greet and talk with them in the first few moments of the session; use activity 2.2: The Interview and activity 2.4: Direct Observation (Systematic/Assess Participant Learning Needs and Styles; see chapter 2).

Prepare the room

The instructor should get to the workshop site at least an hour early to assess the teaching and learning environment. Though the room setup may not take long, unforeseen problems often crop up. Be ready for anything—the room has been double-booked, the chairs are down the hall, or the only key to the room is with the janitor who is home sick; refer to activity 16.1: Early Planning (Safe/Help Participants Feel at Home; see chapter 5).

A room set up as a learning environment can include electronic equipment, a table display of the latest books on child guidance, or handouts related to your topic. You might put posters of children on the walls. You might set up a slide program to play continuously or an overhead projector that displays a saying or an image to pique interest. You can play relaxing music to greet participants. You may wish to arrange chairs in a large circle, or in rows if the activities require participants to move into groups fairly early in the workshop. Refer to activities 16.3: Welcoming Environment, 16.4: Displays, 16.5: Seating, and 16.6: Add Your Special Touch (Safe/Help Participants Feel at Home; see chapter 5).

You will want to post the goals and agenda, including methods you plan to use so participants will know what to expect during the session, using activities 17.1: Share Basic Instructional Information (Safe/Let Participants Know What to Expect; see chapter 5) and 19.5: Publish the Agenda(Safe/Keep Time Commitments; see chapter 5).

Here is what your goals, methods, and agenda might look like for this workshop:

Managing Misbehavior in Children
Workshop Goals

Participants will

- explore and identify misbehavior
- explore and identify causes of misbehavior
- learn and use the AIM approach
- have fun and enjoy the workshop

Methods

Small-group exercises and discussions

Self-disclosure/sharing

Lecturettes

Handouts

Personal reflection

Peer consultation

Agenda

Introduction and warm-up

Explore and identify misbehavior

Break

Explore and identify causes of misbehavior

Learn the AIM approach

Break

Reflection

Peer consultation

Evaluation and wrap-up

Facilitate the workshop

Introduction and warm-up. The instructor reviews the published goals, agenda, and methods. Stress that the workshop involves some personal sharing with others and that the first part of the workshop will involve meeting new people as well as building a small group that will later work together in consultation on real situations they face. Refer to activities 19.5: Publish the Agenda, 17.1: Share Basic Instructional Information, and 17.2: Housekeeping (Safe/Keep Time Commitments; Safe/Let Participants Know What to Expect; see chapter 5).

After sharing this information, it is important for the instructor to solicit questions and comments from the participants, as in activities 1.3 On-the-Spot Collaboration and 3.5 Getting Agreement on Goals (Systematic/Collaborate with Participants As You Plan and Systematic/Set Clear, Meaningful Goals; see chapter 2).

The warm-up and get-acquainted exercise should be designed to develop the group and start the workshop in a fun and nonthreatening way; this plan uses activity 18.1: Tell Your Life Story in One Minute (Safe/Help Participants Get Acquainted; see chapter 5). A good warm-up exercise for those who are already acquainted with each other is "What's on Your Plate?" because it helps people clear the air and begin to focus on the task at hand; refer to activities 14.2: Self-Disclosure and 14.1: Meet New People (Spontaneous/Build in Risk Taking; see chapter 4). The instructor needs to facilitate intimate small-group sharing, which helps participants to tell their stories, as in activities 11.1: Small

Groups and 11.3: Seating Close Together (Spontaneous/Help Participants Tell Their Stories; see chapter 4).

Explore and identify misbehavior. Begin with a definition of misbehavior, but prepare to be flexible with this definition based on the group's response, as in activity 17.7: Be Flexible (Safe/Let Participants Know What to Expect; see chapter 5). Offer a definition such as "misbehavior is child behavior that represents an apparent breach of adult rules, trust, or common sense." Have participants break into small groups and ask them to discuss the definition or come up with their own definitions. Discuss the various definitions, write them on flip-chart sheets, and post them around the room. Next, ask small groups of participants to list all the misbehaviors they most commonly encounter in child care. List misbehaviors on flip-chart sheets placed around the room. This experience may be quite enlightening for caregivers as they realize what a tough job they have. This part of the workshop uses activities 14.2: Self-Disclosure and 14.4: Share Ideas (Spontaneous/Build in Risk Taking; see chapter 4) and activity 7.6: Small Groups and Intergroup Sharing (Stimulating/Use Active Learning Approaches; see chapter 3).

Explore and identify causes of misbehavior. This topic has two parts. First, the small groups are asked to identify what they believe are the causes of misbehavior, using activities 7.6: Small Groups and Intergroup Sharing and 8.1: Remembering (Stimulating/Use Active Learning Approaches and Encourage Creativity; see chapter 3).

Second, the instructor provides a framework for classifying these causes. The particular way of classifying the behaviors listed in Table 7-3 is not the only way. There are many theories and models for understanding and classifying behavior—any reasonable model will do. The important point is that knowing something about the causes leads to better solutions; this workshop delivers information by using activities 6.1: The Lecturette and 6.3: Visual Aids (Stimulating/Present Information in Interesting, Useful Ways; see chapter 3).

As participants work together within the small groups, they are forming good consultation teams for later in the workshop; refer to activity 20.5: Working and Playing Together (Safe/Build Trust and Openness; see chapter 5).

TABLE 7-3

Some Possible Causes of Misbehavior

Chronic Issues

Organic—including attention deficit disorders, fetal alcohol syndrome, chemical imbalance, and disease.

Substance misuse or abuse—including illegal drug use by child or parent, exposure to environments where drugs are abused.

Adjustment—including post-traumatic stress syndrome, childhood trauma, dysfunctional or marginal families.

Developmental—including ages and stages, immaturity.

Periodic Issues

Reactions to events—including insecurities, fears, anger, disappointment in response to divorce, death, or changes in the family or child care.

Reactions to environments—including insecurities, fears, anger, disappointment in response to a mismatch of child and caregiver, caregiver attention level, child grouping, transitions.

Values clash—including power struggles, personal preferences, arguments, fights.

Accidents—including misjudgments, miscalculations, missed schedules.

Learn the AIM approach. There are many models for working with child guidance in child care settings, but this one is offered as an example. For an overview, see the AIM Approach handout (Table 7-4). Have participants break into small groups and ask them to describe a situation in which a child demonstrates chronic misbehavior. Ask the group to address the problem using the AIM approach. Have each small group share the situation and solutions in the large group, using activity 10.6: Small Group of Peers (Stimulating/Help Participants Practice New Learning; see chapter 3).

TABLE 7-4

The AIM Approach

A= Actual Behavior

Determine and describe all possible and plausible causes of misbehavior. One method proceeds as follows:

1. Observe the child's behavior, what happens just before and just after, and look for patterns.
2. Listen actively and give attention to the nonverbal as well as the verbal clues.
3. Interview parents or teachers or, with proper permission, others who know and understand the child.
4. Consult with experts (with proper permission) such as social workers, therapists, child psychologists, or other providers.
5. Search books, articles, or the Internet for pertinent information.
6. Review records, the child's file, notes you have made, or other documents that might give you insight.
7. Think the situation through and make a list of ideas.
8. Record special notes to help you look for patterns.
9. Based on the steps above, write a brief narrative describing the situation and possible causes.

I = Ideal

Think about what may be the best result for the child or situation in question. How will you know when the problem is solved? Briefly describe a reachable, relevant goal.

M = Method

Put together a plan to reach the goal you have described. Below are some activities that can help you reach your stated goals.

- Use rule—provide clear limits.
- Use reason—provide consistency.
- Use relationships—control through caring.
- Use reinforcement—confirm and guide.
- Use resources and referrals.

Reflection. Provide a few minutes for participants to think about their child care situation and child guidance issues, as in activity 15.6: Thought Stimulators (Spontaneous/Take Time to Reflect; see chapter 4).

Peer consultation. The small groups for this activity have already worked together. The instructor asks participants to transform their group into a consultation team and spend time sharing child misbehavior and child guidance issues as they consult with one another, as in activity 9.2: Participant Consultants (Stimulating/Help Participants Solve Real Problems; see chapter 3). The instructor can join a group or "float" and be available to assist, using activities 11.1: Small Groups and 11.2: Small Groups Over a Longer Time (Spontaneous/Help Participants Tell Their Stories; see chapter 4).

The participants should also be encouraged to write intervention plans as a rehearsal for the real-life events they will face in their own child care setting, as in activity 10.1: Plan, Write, and Review (Stimulating/Help Participants Practice New Learning; see chapter 3).

Evaluation and wrap-up. When the consultation is over, reassemble the large group and solicit comments and questions. Provide copies of the evaluation form (see Table 7-5). After tabulating the ratings and reading over the comments, the instructor can modify and improve the workshop presentation based on this information (Systematic Strategy 5: Evaluate Your Plan; see the discussion of questionnaires on page 33).

TABLE 7-5

Workshop Evaluation Form
"Managing Misbehavior in Children"

Rate to what extent the workshop has met each of the goals below.
(1 = little, 2 = some, 3 = much, 4 = very much)

1. Explore and identify misbehavior.	1	2	3	4
2. Explore and identify causes of misbehavior.	1	2	3	4
3. Learn and use the AIM approach.	1	2	3	4
4. Have fun and enjoy the workshop.	1	2	3	4

List some things you liked about this workshop:

_____

_____

_____

_____

_____

List some things that might be changed:

_____

_____

_____

_____

_____

Your message to the instructor:

_____

_____

_____

_____

_____

Summary

The sample workshop and the references to the corresponding instructor styles, strategies, and learning activities should provide you with an idea of how to apply the Teach with Style model. A summary of the Teach with Style model is in the appendix. The information in this appendix provides a quick overview for first-time instructors as well as for experienced teachers of adults. As you learn and use the model, and as you plan for your continuous improvement, you will find that your effectiveness in teaching adults will grow. The next chapter will help you evaluate your teaching skills so that you can build on your strengths and work on areas that need improvement.

Plan your continuous improvement

We are creatures of habit, and necessarily so. The routines and patterns we form give us the freedom to concentrate on the unpredictable aspects of our lives. We put much of our lives on autopilot, a tactic that helps us survive an endlessly changing world. Our need to create patterns of thinking and behaving has a downside, however. When we are called upon to be creative, respond to unique situations, or learn new behavior, these rigid patterns may hinder us from developing unique or creative responses.

How do we break out of our molds, change, and adapt to meet unique problems? We are often able to change and adapt when we are forced by circumstances to do so. We also alter our set ways when we are *affirmed*—that is, when we are so secure in our own sense of self that we are willing to take a look at our beliefs and behaviors and see the need for improvement or change. Affirmation can be expressed as self-esteem, self-actualization, confidence, belief in one's ultimate worth, being centered, and so on. These states of being are infrequently realized, but they are goals toward which we strive.

A family child care provider was once threatened with legal action by a licensing agency because of some major deficiencies. This provider was very defensive about the problems, because she felt threatened. The licenser quickly became aware of her fears and offered to help by referring her to child care education classes. This provider had spent years developing poor child care habits, but when she found herself facing legal action she made the effort to take the classes. In her classes she found some supportive fellow participants and an instructor who was accepting and helpful. She made significant changes in her behavior as a result of the classes and received affirmation from the participants and instructor as she struggled with change.

As an instructor of adults, you may find that you have some well-worn ways of teaching. These ways may be just fine, but you should explore other ways as well. If you are reading this section on continuous improvement, you must be having some thoughts about how to be a better teacher. Already, if you have read the previous chapters, you know that a balanced approach is best, and that you should apply all four of the instructor styles equally when teaching adults. If you strive for that balance, you will be on a path toward continuous improvement. To make progress you must (1) become aware of how you teach, (2) make a commitment to change, and (3) try out new instructional strategies and learning activities.

Accepting and acting on helpful criticism

In the children's story "The Emperor's New Clothes," an emperor imagines he has wonderful new clothes but is, in fact, completely naked. No one, except an innocent child, dares to tell him the truth. Avoiding criticism is one sure way to get mired in rigidity, but it is quite a normal reaction. We tend not to notice painful truths about ourselves. It may be especially difficult to accept critical remarks as an instructor.

The aim of *Teach with Style* is to challenge instructors to make continuous improvement. That means accepting a critical view of your work and then changing accordingly. Of course, there are many ways to teach. It is important that you are affirmed as you bring your unique slant to the role of teacher. So consider the changes you make as building on your strengths. Find a good balance between pushing yourself to change and appreciating yourself as you are.

Two errors in receiving feedback

The first error in receiving feedback is to seek only affirmation and avoid negative feedback. When you get feedback forms from a group of participants, you may be tempted to sort through them to find the good comments and high marks and pay little attention to the criticism. The second error is to dwell on the few negative comments and miss the positive comments. Even one harsh-sounding comment may hold you captive. Don't get bogged down and miss the good comments. Naturally, a balanced approach is best.

Celebrate your strengths as reflected in complimentary statements and accolades, but take an objective and open posture when examining where you need to improve.

How we accept criticism is often based on our experience of being criticized in the past. Helpful criticism begins with noticing strengths and works best when we have to ask for it rather than when it is uninvited. Helpful criticism points out specific strengths or errors rather than offering general praise or rebuke. Taking a critical look at yourself is never easy. If you are resistant to constructive criticism based on accurate feedback, you will not achieve continuous improvement. Step back and see what you could do to make realistic changes.

Inventories as tools for continuous improvement

This chapter offers inventories and a process for continuous improvement. The following steps will help you improve as you teach.

1. Begin by learning your instructor style, using the Instructor Style Inventory. After completing this inventory, review all of the instructor styles and strategies.

2. Use the Instructor Self-Assessment Inventory to assess what strategies you need to strengthen or use more often.

3. Ask the people who attend your workshops or classes to use the Participant Inventory; use their responses to assess how participants experience your instruction.

4. Invite an observer to use the Observer Inventory for further analysis.

5. Finally, you are ready to plan your improvement. Try using the Instructor Continuous Improvement Worksheet and the AIM process.

This process becomes a cycle of improvement when it is used repeatedly in your effort to become a better teacher. (See Continuous Improvement Cycle, Table 8-1.)

TABLE 8-1

The Teach with Style
Continuous Improvement Cycle

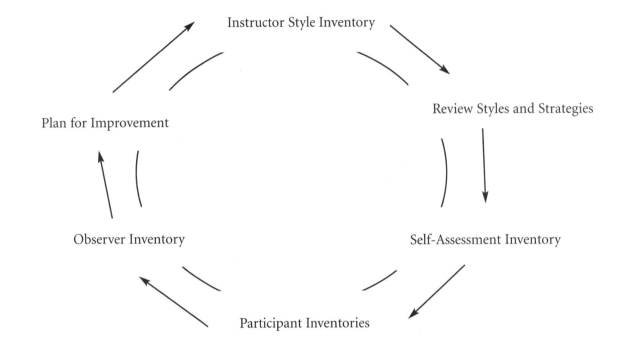

Instructor Style Inventory

Plan for Improvement

Review Styles and Strategies

Observer Inventory

Self-Assessment Inventory

Participant Inventories

Instructor assessment inventories

The instructor assessment inventories are listed in Table 8-2. You are encouraged to use the inventories in this section often, particularly the participant inventories. These tools guide your continual improvement. Getting critical responses from different points of view is helpful. How do you, as the teacher, perceive your styles and strategies? How do your participants experience your instruction? How does a supervisor or colleague assess your work? You get a well-rounded and accurate picture with assessments from these three perspectives.

Pay attention to both negative and positive feedback. Do not dwell on one participant's negative comment while ignoring the good that was experienced by the other participants. On the other hand, remember not to hungrily absorb praise while ignoring valuable criticism. You should look for general

TABLE 8-2

Summary of Instructor Assessment Inventories

Table and Page #	Inventory	Purpose
Table 8-3A, B, C, D (Pages 132–136)	Instructor Style Inventory	Identifies your unique blend of the four instructor styles. Suggests how to make improvements for a more balanced approach.
Table 8-4 (Page 137)	Instructor Self-Assessment Inventory	Assesses how much you use each of the twenty strategies. Helps you select the strategies you want to improve.
Table 8-5 (Page 138)	Participant Inventory: Instructor Styles	Helps you assess how a participant experiences your instruction. The focus is on the four styles and serves as a "quick check" of your styles.
Table 8-6 (Page 139)	Participant Inventory: Instructor Strategies	Helps you assess how a participant experiences your instruction. The focus is on your use of the twenty strategies.
Table 8-7 (Pages 140–144)	Observer Inventory	Provides an observer with a tool to assess your instruction. Gives you specific evidence of how you use strategies. Helps you identify specific areas for improvement.
Table 8-8 (Page 146)	Instructor Continuous Improvement Worksheet	Provides step-by-step analysis of inventory results and helps you plan for improvement.

clues that point you toward improving performance and balancing styles. Look for consistent and persistent remarks that point to your pattern of instruction, and let these guide your actions.

Take a moment to review all of the assessment inventories so that you are aware of the various viewpoints from which you can seek assessment of your strengths and weaknesses as a teacher.

TABLE 8-3A

Instructor Style Inventory—Instructions

Follow the steps to determine your instructor style, then read the interpretation pages that follow.

Step One: Read through the list on the next page and rate each personal characteristic as follows:

Exactly describes me = 10

Somewhat or sometimes describes me = 5

This is not very descriptive of me = 0

(PLEASE USE ONLY 0, 5, OR 10)

Hint: It may be helpful to think of yourself in the instructional role as you fill out the inventory. If you have not been an instructor yet, then rate yourself as if you were an instructor—use your imagination.

TABLE 8-3B

Instructor Style Inventory—Rating Sheet

	Rate	Characteristic		Rate	Characteristic
1.	_____	Caring toward others	25.	_____	Soothing personality
2.	_____	Challenges others to improve	26.	_____	Feels confident
3.	_____	Playful	27.	_____	Unpredictable—a little wild
4.	_____	Very logical	28.	_____	Likes to do research
5.	_____	Sympathetic toward others	29.	_____	Sensitive to others' feelings
6.	_____	Considered charismatic	30.	_____	Immovable in beliefs
7.	_____	Silly	31.	_____	Considered an engaging person
8.	_____	Realistic, level-headed	32.	_____	Evaluates situations
9.	_____	Good listener to all	33.	_____	Concerned for comfort of others
10.	_____	Very intuitive	34.	_____	Persuasive—influences others
11.	_____	Considered lively and fun	35.	_____	Creative or inventive
12.	_____	Analytically driven	36.	_____	Likes being accountable
13.	_____	Peacemaker	37.	_____	Accepting of others
14.	_____	Makes things happen	38.	_____	Lives by principles
15.	_____	Funny	39.	_____	Active and lively
16.	_____	Thorough	40.	_____	Considered very sensible
17.	_____	Serves others	41.	_____	Relaxes others
18.	_____	Dynamic leader	42.	_____	Motivates people to act
19.	_____	Likes to tell stories	43.	_____	Delightful
20.	_____	Purposeful in approach	44.	_____	Likes clear rules and routines
21.	_____	Likes to put people at ease	45.	_____	Comforts others
22.	_____	Takes charge	46.	_____	Confronting comes easy
23.	_____	Considered a party animal	47.	_____	Tends to lose track of time
24.	_____	Good planner	48.	_____	Keeps things right on track

TABLE 8-3C

Instructor Style Inventory—Score Sheet

Step Two: Transfer your scores from the Rating Sheet (page 133) to the appropriate blanks below, and then fill in the total rating score for each style.

Rating	Number	Rating	Number	Rating	Number	Rating	Number
_____	1.	_____	2.	_____	3.	_____	4.
_____	5.	_____	6.	_____	7.	_____	8.
_____	9.	_____	10.	_____	11.	_____	12.
_____	13.	_____	14.	_____	15.	_____	16.
_____	17.	_____	18.	_____	19.	_____	20.
_____	21.	_____	22.	_____	23.	_____	24.
_____	25.	_____	26.	_____	27.	_____	28.
_____	29.	_____	30.	_____	31.	_____	32.
_____	33.	_____	34.	_____	35.	_____	36.
_____	37.	_____	38.	_____	39.	_____	40.
_____	41.	_____	42.	_____	43.	_____	44.
_____	45.	_____	46.	_____	47.	_____	48.
_____ Total		_____ Total		_____ Total		_____ Total	
SAFE		STIMULATING		SPONTANEOUS		SYSTEMATIC	

Step Three: After calculating your instructor style rating, read the Interpretation section of this inventory (page 135).

Step Four: Enter the information on the Instructor Continuous Improvement Worksheet (Table 8-8).

TABLE 8-3D

Instructor Style Inventory—Interpretation

The Instructor Style Inventory is most helpful when instructors find their greatest strengths clearly identified. You may discover that yours fall equally into all four of the instructor styles, or your results may show no clear area of strength. You may have a balance in all four areas. If this is true for you, it may be helpful to read the following descriptions and choose the instructor style you most want to develop. This inventory is a guide for continuous improvement; it is not meant as a scientific determination of your strengths or weaknesses as an instructor, nor is it a validated personality inventory.

Safe

DESCRIPTION: The instructor who scores in the high range of the safe style makes sure adult participants feel at ease and comfortable. Visual evidence of this is found in a relaxed seating arrangement and welcome signs or posters that invite the participants in. Refreshments and name tags are prepared. The instructor makes an effort to be personable and sensitive to each participant, and he helps participants build trust with warm-up experiences. Expectations are clear and participants have some control over the way the class develops.

CRITERIA FOR SUCCESS: Participants have warm feelings about each other and about the learning experience.

FINDING BALANCE: This instructor may tend to pay too little attention to confrontation with participants. He may be so concerned about participants' comfort that vital knowledge and skill may be overlooked. To find balance, look to the Stimulating Instructor Style for strategies to challenge participants to think, change, and grow.

Stimulating

DESCRIPTION: The instructor who scores in the high range of the stimulating style challenges and motivates participants. She uses active learning methods and focuses on real problems that participants face. Key principles are presented in interesting and lively ways and participants are expected to grasp and rely on them. This teacher confronts participants with new ideas, and she wants them to understand and change. This instructor takes participants on a fascinating, stimulating, and persuasive trip toward greater awareness.

CRITERIA FOR SUCCESS: Participants have a solid core of new understanding, knowledge, and skills they can apply.

FINDING BALANCE: This instructor may pay too little attention to the feelings and personal needs of adult participants. A persuasive personality and focus on confrontation may jeopardize the instructor's ability to help participants make positive change because she lacks sensitivity to participant needs. To find balance, look to the Safe Instructor Style for strategies to build a protective atmosphere where adults can risk change.

TABLE 8-3D

Instructor Style Inventory—Interpretation, continued

Systematic

DESCRIPTION: The instructor who scores in the high range of the systematic style wants the learning experience orderly, proceeding from carefully constructed objectives. A key to this style is identifying adult styles and needs. This instructor directs the educational endeavor from well-researched information and logical thought followed by rational steps toward a defined end. He wants the participants to understand why and how the instruction is designed and seeks cooperation to achieve the desired objectives. There is little room for extraneous material in the planned path toward knowledge and competent performance.

CRITERIA FOR SUCCESS: Participants follow an orderly process toward the agreed-on learning goals and tasks.

FINDING BALANCE: Although the instruction may be well organized, the experience might not be very engaging and enjoyable for adult participants. If participants lose interest, they may just go through the motions to meet expectations. Cold, logical plans and procedures may lose their impact without a little fun and surprise. To find balance, look to the Spontaneous Instructor Style for strategies for play, humor, and surprise that promote freedom and discovery.

Spontaneous

DESCRIPTION: The instructor who scores in the high range of the spontaneous style uses humor, interaction, and stories to motivate and engage participants. This instructor likes to see learners having fun. The more animated the conversations and debates the better. A lively discussion in large or small groups is vital to this teaching style. Jokes and humor are added to keep the interest high. Surprise and serendipity encourage discovery learning. This teacher gets people interacting and processing in small groups. She is enthusiastic and finds interesting and surprising ways to involve the learners.

CRITERIA FOR SUCCESS: Participants laugh and enjoy themselves while discovering new ideas.

FINDING BALANCE: All that enthusiasm, humor, and activity can turn off the serious participant. There is a danger of being too cute and gimmicky. A bad joke can ruin a relationship and stymie learning. Participants may have a good time, but necessary learning could be lost without careful planning. To find balance, look to the Systematic Instructor Style for strategies for logical planning toward clear, agreed-on goals and tasks.

TABLE 8-4

Instructor Self-Assessment Inventory

Name: _____ **Date:** _____

After you thoroughly review the instructor styles and strategies in this book, rate how much you use the strategies listed below.

Key:

    1 = Never use this strategy

    2 = Seldom use this strategy

    3 = Sometimes use this strategy

    4 = Frequently use this strategy

    5 = Always use this strategy

    NA = Not applicable in my teaching

Make It Systematic:

____ Collaborate with participants as you plan.

____ Assess participant learning needs and styles.

____ Set clear, meaningful goals.

____ Plan to reach your goals.

____ Evaluate your plan.

Make It Stimulating:

____ Present information in interesting, useful ways.

____ Use active learning approaches.

____ Encourage creativity.

____ Help participants solve real problems.

____ Help participants practice new learning.

Make It Spontaneous:

____ Help participants tell their stories.

____ Make it funny, make it fun.

____ Use imagination and the arts.

____ Build in risk taking.

____ Take time to reflect.

Make It Safe:

____ Help participants feel at home.

____ Let participants know what to expect.

____ Help participants get acquainted.

____ Keep time commitments.

____ Build trust and openness.

Go back over the strategies and mark the ones you want to begin improving and using more.

Table 8-5

Participant Inventory: Instructor Styles

Name of Session: _____ **Date:** _____

Name of Instructor(s): _____

Help the instructor(s) make improvements by completing this form. Rate to what extent the four conditions (safe, stimulating, systematic, and spontaneous) were present in this session.

Please circle the number that best fits.

	LITTLE		SOME		MUCH

The instruction was:

Safe

I felt relaxed and comfortable,
and I quickly became involved
with other participants.   1   2   3   4   5

Stimulating

I was actively challenged to learn
new ideas or skills that I can apply.   1   2   3   4   5

Systematic

A clear, logical teaching plan
was explained and followed.   1   2   3   4   5

Spontaneous

There was a free flow of ideas,
humor, and fun.   1   2   3   4   5

What did you like best about this instruction? _____

_____

Suggestions to improve the instruction: _____

_____

Other comments for the instructor(s): _____

_____

TABLE 8-6

Participant Inventory: Instructor Strategies

Name of Session: _____ **Date:** _____

Name of Instructor(s): _____

Instructions: The purpose of this assessment is to help the instructor(s) improve. You will evaluate the strategies used by the instructor(s). Circle the number that best represents your opinion of the instruction you received.

	LITTLE		SOME		MUCH
SAFE					
1. The learning space was comfortable.	1	2	3	4	5
2. We were well aware of what to expect.	1	2	3	4	5
3. We had time to warm up and get acquainted.	1	2	3	4	5
4. The instructor kept to the agreed-on schedule.	1	2	3	4	5
5. Learning tasks enabled us to open up and get close.	1	2	3	4	5
STIMULATING					
6. I was challenged with new ideas I can use.	1	2	3	4	5
7. We were actively engaged in learning activities.	1	2	3	4	5
8. We were encouraged to be creative.	1	2	3	4	5
9. We solved real and important problems we face.	1	2	3	4	5
10. We practiced the new knowledge and skills.	1	2	3	4	5
SYSTEMATIC					
11. The participants helped plan the instruction.	1	2	3	4	5
12. Instruction was based on our needs and learning styles.	1	2	3	4	5
13. The goals of the class were clear and made sense.	1	2	3	4	5
14. I felt that I learned what I needed and wanted.	1	2	3	4	5
15. Participants evaluated the instruction.	1	2	3	4	5
SPONTANEOUS					
16. We worked together in small groups.	1	2	3	4	5
17. We enjoyed ourselves, laughed, and had fun.	1	2	3	4	5
18. We used our imagination or artistic expression.	1	2	3	4	5
19. The instructor helped us take risks to learn.	1	2	3	4	5
20. There was time for thoughtful reflection.	1	2	3	4	5

TABLE 8-7

Observer Inventory

How to use the Observer Inventory:

This Observer Inventory is to be used by "invitation only." Invite an observer to provide feedback to be used for the purpose of instructor self-improvement.

The Observer Inventory is used in conjunction with the Instructor Self-Assessment Inventory on page 137. Both the observer and the instructor must be familiar with the instructor styles and strategies explained in this book.

The instructor and observer must proceed based on mutual trust, understanding of the concepts, and agreement about the purpose of the observation.

The observer needs to see the instructor "in action" and, if possible, observe multiple sessions or sessions longer than one hour. Watch for consistent use of the strategies and the balance of each of the styles: safe, stimulating, systematic, and spontaneous. Circle the appropriate number for each skill observed. Make liberal use of space for evidence (specific behaviors used), comments, and the narrative section.

Spend time discussing the results together so the instructor can plan future sessions with this feedback as a guide for improvement.

Repeat the observation and feedback cycle as often as you like for continuous improvement.

TABLE 8-7

Observer Inventory, continued

Session Title: _____ **Date:** _____

Time: _____ **Place:** _____

Instructor: _____ **Observed by:** _____

Rating: 1 = little, 3 = some, 5 = much, or NA = not applicable

MAKE IT SAFE:

1. The learning space helped participants feel relaxed and welcome.
   Rating: _____

   Evidence: _____

   Comments: _____

2. Participants were able to discuss and negotiate the objectives, methods, schedule, and content.
   Rating: _____

   Evidence: _____

   Comments: _____

3. There was time to warm up so adults could get to know each other and the instructor, and to develop an interest in the topic.
   Rating: _____

   Evidence: _____

   Comments: _____

4. The instructor kept to the schedule as agreed or renegotiated.
   Rating: _____

   Evidence: _____

   Comments: _____

5. Participants had a sense of closeness with others and were able to share concerns and help others solve problems.
   Rating: _____

   Evidence: _____

   Comments: _____

Total Rating for Safe _____

TABLE 8-7

Observer Inventory, continued

MAKE IT STIMULATING:

6. Participants indicated that they were gaining new insights and finding solutions they plan to use.

Rating: _____

Evidence: _____

Comments: _____

7. Participants were involved in active learning tasks at least 50 percent of the time.

Rating: _____

Evidence: _____

Comments: _____

8. Participants were able to create, experiment with, and try out new ways of thinking and acting.

Rating: _____

Evidence: _____

Comments: _____

9. Participants were engaged in solving real and important problems that they face.

Rating: _____

Evidence: _____

Comments: _____

10. Participants were able to practice knowledge and skill and receive feedback on their progress.

Rating: _____

Evidence: _____

Comments: _____

Total Rating for Stimulating _____

TABLE 8-7

Observer Inventory, continued

MAKE IT SYSTEMATIC:

11. The instruction was well targeted and flexible in meeting participant needs.

    Rating: _____

    Evidence: _____

    Comments: _____

12. The instruction was based on participant needs, interests, learning styles, and diversity issues.

    Rating: _____

    Evidence: _____

    Comments: _____

13. Participants were accurately informed about learning goals, objectives, and methods.

    Rating: _____

    Evidence: _____

    Comments: _____

14. Participants indicated that they learned what they needed and wanted.

    Rating: _____

    Evidence: _____

    Comments: _____

15. Participants received information about the overall effectiveness of the program.

    Rating: _____

    Evidence: _____

    Comments: _____

Total Rating for Systematic _____

TABLE 8-7

Observer Inventory, continued

MAKE IT SPONTANEOUS:

16. An important part of the session content was gained through participants' sharing their knowledge and experience.

    Rating: _____

    Evidence: _____

    Comments: _____

17. There was opportunity for playfulness; participants laughed and enjoyed themselves.

    Rating: _____

    Evidence: _____

    Comments: _____

18. Participants experienced creative expression as a factor leading to positive change.

    Rating: _____

    Evidence: _____

    Comments: _____

19. The instructor promoted an attitude of risk taking and modeled willingness to change.

    Rating: _____

    Evidence: _____

    Comments: _____

20. Time was made for silence, quiet reflection, and journaling to integrate new ideas.

    Rating: _____

    Evidence: _____

    Comments: _____

Total Rating for Spontaneous _____

A = Actual. The first step is to identify and describe how you are actually doing right now. What are your strengths and weaknesses? If you have already identified some areas for improvement, focus on these. If you have used the instructor feedback inventories mentioned earlier, you should be able to make one or more statements that will be your baseline. For example, "I have been planning my sessions without adequately assessing the needs and interests of my participants."

I = Ideal. Consider how you want things to be. Use your actual statements as a guide for setting your goals. Be specific about what you want. If you use one instructor style more than another or do not use all the strategies consistently, you may want to focus on greater balance. Make it your goal to strengthen the styles and strategies you use less often. You may want to begin by selecting just one area for improvement. Write one or more goal statements. For example, "I want to accurately assess the learning needs of my participants before each workshop I teach."

M = Method. The final step is to select methods that will get you from the actual to the ideal. Use the ideal statements to create your plan for improvement. Make one or more statements that will describe your plan. For example, "I will consult several training or adult education books and articles and find ten good ways to assess participant needs and interests. I will use the best methods consistently over the next six months."

Use the Instructor Continuous Improvement Worksheet (Table 8-8) as a resource to help you plan your improvement. The Instructor Continuous Improvement Worksheet guides you through the AIM process and asks you to record the information from inventories and to make some decisions about your continuous improvement.

TABLE 8-8

Instructor Continuous Improvement Worksheet

Your Name: _____ **Date:** _____

A = Actual

1. Instructor Style

Instructor Style Inventory scores:

Safe _____   Stimulating _____   Spontaneous _____   Systematic _____

Summarize your Participant Inventory: Instructor Styles results: _____

Summarize your style(s) in your own words: _____

What style(s) do you need to learn to gain better balance in instruction?

_____

2. Instructor Strategies

Summarize your Instructor Self-Assessment Inventory results: _____

List the strategies you use most: _____

List strategies you want or need to learn to use more: _____

_____

Summarize your Participant Inventory: Instructor Strategies results: _____

What strategies do participants indicate you use most? _____

_____

What strategies do participants indicate you use least? _____

_____

Summarize your Observer Inventory results: _____

What strategies does the observer indicate you use most? _____

_____

What strategies did the observer indicate you use least? _____

_____

Summary of A = Actual

Make one or more statements that focus on areas in your instruction that need improvement.

_____

I = Ideal

Set Goals for Improvement: Make parallel statements to the actual statements above that describe how you want your instruction to be improved. Which of these I = Ideal statements are most important to you right now? Mark those as key for targeting your M = Method statements.

M = Method

Plan to Improve: Make one or more statements that describe what you will do to accomplish the ideal. Methods I will use for improving my instruction:

- Statement _____ Target Date: _____
- Statement _____ Target Date: _____
- Statement _____ Target Date: _____

Ten ideas for self-development

The following ideas will get you thinking about plans for continuous improvement as an instructor.

- Reading lists: Develop a reading list of books, journals, and other sources that you can study to develop each strategy. Create a resource file or notebook with new ideas.
- Support group: Meet with other instructors and develop a small support group to work toward improvement.
- Training: Search for training sessions that fit your needs and attend them.
- Self-directed development: Conduct your own specific needs assessment; set a specific set of objectives; plan your own practice and feedback; and create an evaluation of your plan.
- Expert consultation: Do you know someone who has much skill and experience in the strategy you want to develop? Seek out that person and contract for consultation, mentoring, or coaching.
- Multimedia presentations: Search for audio, CD, or video presentations and rent, borrow, or purchase these.
- Brainstorm and create: Sit down with others or go on a personal mini-retreat to devise, create, and invent ideas that will help you develop the strategy you need.
- Buddy system: Remember your swimming lessons as a kid? Find another person who wants to learn the same strategy you do and form a pact to learn together and support each other.
- Consult participants: You can gain much insight by asking your participants to propose ways you can improve. Make a special effort to spend time whenever possible to get ideas and feedback from your participants. Ask them many questions, and listen carefully.
- Professional association: When you join professional organizations, the emphasis is usually on improving knowledge and skills. You will receive a journal, invitations to conferences, and resources for improving your practice.

Summary

The continuous improvement process, the instructor inventories, and the planning worksheet provide you with ways to gain insight into your weaknesses and strengths as an instructor. These tools are provided as a means for improving your instruction, but of course the time and effort you put into it will determine your success. If you use these tools conscientiously, your adult participants will benefit from them too.

The Teach with Style model offers all of the elements you need to become a confident, competent instructor. The styles, strategies, and learning activities, as well as the sample workshops, provide a hands-on guide to help you design and implement balanced, effective instruction. Tools for continuous improvement guarantee your ongoing effectiveness in teaching adults.

Summary of the Teach with Style model, styles, and strategies

The information in this appendix provides a quick overview of the Teach with Style model. Instructors who are teaching for the first time, as well as those who have taught adult participants frequently, can use the following information as a refresher course in concepts key to the Teach with Style model.

The nature and importance of strategies

The four instructor *styles*—systematic, spontaneous, stimulating, and safe—are implemented using twenty specific *strategies*. As you study the strategies, begin to identify those you tend to avoid or use less often. The strategies you seldom use are most likely those you should use and improve. The key is to provide a balanced application of all four styles. You will teach more effectively and serve your participants better.

Most instructors, including beginners, have a natural talent for using some of the strategies. Learning and practice will help beginning teachers master other strategies, which in turn will improve their performance. Experienced instructors can use the Teach with Style model to tune up some areas.

Instructor strategies are the building blocks for each instructor style. They are the ways you create necessary conditions for learning. They guide the specific learning activities and techniques you use as you design and implement effective learning. In fact, the particular cluster of strategies used to influence participants is what determines an instructor's style. Instructors with a balanced and broad range of strategies are most effective. They are sensitive observers who are able to adjust their instruction to the unique and diverse needs of adult participants. Instructors who use a balanced teaching style are able to help participants become motivated, open to change, and consequently better prepared for life and work. Below are brief descriptions of the instructor styles and strategies with some examples.

Make instruction systematic

Adults learn more when they participate in well-planned programs that are cooperatively designed. Systematic instruction is characterized by shared goals, a program that reaches the goals, and evaluation of progress toward the goals. The systematic strategies and learning activities will help you design instruction so it flows logically from learning needs to learning outcomes.

Systematic strategies include the following:

- Strategy 1—Collaborate with participants as you plan
- Strategy 2—Assess participant learning needs and styles
- Strategy 3—Set clear, meaningful goals
- Strategy 4—Plan to reach your goals
- Strategy 5—Evaluate your plan

Systematic strategies

1. COLLABORATE WITH PARTICIPANTS AS YOU PLAN. The instruction should be well targeted and flexible in meeting participant needs. To the greatest possible extent, consult participants or their representatives as you plan. Involve participants before and during the course of instruction to make the experience relevant to their needs. Be willing to shift the program when warranted, and let participants share in the consequences of outcomes.

Learning is enhanced when participants take ownership of the learning experience. You collaborate with them when you meet directly with a group of participants early on to involve them in planning, or when you ask them to conduct the learning experience. You can also use a guided focus group in which you meet with representative participants to identify learning needs. Plan the program after participant needs have been listed and prioritized.

2. ASSESS PARTICIPANT LEARNING NEEDS AND STYLES. The instruction should be based on participant needs, interests, and styles of learning. Diversity issues must be considered. Pay attention to the accessibility of facilities, to special learning needs, and to anti-bias concerns. Determine how participants best receive, integrate, and express information.

You can assess learning needs when you get acquainted with your participants, discover their learning needs and desires, and respond to them.

3. **SET CLEAR, MEANINGFUL GOALS.** Carefully formulate and articulate goals and objectives that are compatible with the needs and interests of participants. Make these available for review by participants. Participants appreciate it when an instructor tells them specifically what they can expect to gain by attending the workshop. Sometimes specific behavioral objectives and benefits are helpful, for example, "You will be able to diaper a baby in a safe and sanitary way." Sometimes more general goals and benefits are helpful, for example, "You will feel more relaxed in the child care setting." Whether goals are specific or general, tell participants how they will benefit from the instruction.

4. **PLAN TO REACH YOUR GOALS.** Provide a program that is based on and achieves the objectives. If necessary, be willing to renegotiate with participants to adjust the program or goals. When the program is completed, the participants should report in the evaluation whether they learned what they needed and wanted. If you tell participants they will learn to diaper a baby in a safe and sanitary way, make sure that is what participants can do by the end of the workshop. What happens in the instruction should match precisely the stated objectives, goals, or purpose.

5. **EVALUATE YOUR PLAN.** Assess the degree to which the program meets the objectives and make this information available to the participants. Make suggestions if future training is needed. Evaluating whether or not participants can follow the steps to safe and sanitary diapering is relatively easy. Evaluating the effects of instruction on a complex topic such as caregiver stress takes more finesse. Whether simple or complex, results should be evaluated in order to increase the effectiveness of your instruction.

Make instruction stimulating

Stimulating instruction motivates adults to learn and to make positive changes as they encounter ideas presented in interesting and lively ways. This style provokes and challenges participants to change attitudes and behavior. Information is presented in ways that engage participants and make them think.

Stimulating strategies include the following:

- Strategy 6—Present information in interesting, useful ways

- Strategy 7—Use active learning approaches
- Strategy 8—Encourage creativity
- Strategy 9—Help participants solve real problems
- Strategy 10—Help participants practice new learning

Stimulating strategies

6. **Present information in interesting, useful ways.** Participants should gain new insights and find new solutions they can use and apply in their work settings after the workshop is over. They need new perspectives and fresh ways to cope, because adults tend to think and act in familiar and rigid patterns. Instructors must encourage adults to change both by challenging the old and by introducing the new as a valid alternative.

7. **Use active learning approaches.** Experienced instructors know that adults learn by doing, not by hearing someone talk at them. Variety is the spice of life *and* of learning. Adults should be actively involved in learning tasks at least 50 percent of the time. Use a variety of methods that engage visual, aural, kinesthetic, emotional, cognitive, creative, and reflective responses. Didactic presentations should always be balanced with experiential learning. The more you can involve all aspects of participants' personalities, the better they will comprehend and retain new information or skills.

8. **Encourage creativity.** Adults should be engaged in creating and experimenting with new knowledge and strategies to foster change and growth. Help them invent, originate, conceive, author, and express their creativity by removing their fear and ambivalence. Present a process that helps adults take the creative risk. Help participants create personal action plans by providing a few essential concepts that will organize their thoughts and provide just enough structure to free the mind and help generate new ideas. You provide the categories, and they provide the creative thinking.

9. **Help participants solve real problems.** Adults should be engaged in solving important and relevant problems. Problem-solving techniques can be taught and used to reinforce the course content. Encourage participants to work on decisions or issues that they face in their daily lives. Learning will occur when the learning task is closely related to the problems to be solved by participants.

10. **Help participants practice new learning.** Participants should be able to try out new behaviors. Provide a way for participants to practice and receive feedback by being evaluated on their grasp of concepts or strategies being taught. Give participants an opportunity to rehearse strategies they may be called upon to perform in the future. Help adults feel prepared. Honest and fair evaluation reinforces the need to continually assess and improve, which is true for both instructors and participants.

Make instruction spontaneous

Spontaneity in instruction gives adult participants opportunities and permission to try out new ways of seeing. They need a new slant on things. Help them break free from old patterns. Unpredictability fosters the process of freeing adults from the same old lines of thinking. Plan and allow for play, humor, and surprise in your instruction. When adults play, laugh, and take risks together, the walls of resistance weaken and fall.

Spontaneous strategies include the following:
- Strategy 11—Help participants tell their stories
- Strategy 12—Make it funny, make it fun
- Strategy 13—Use imagination and the arts
- Strategy 14—Build in risk taking
- Strategy 15—Take time to reflect

Spontaneous strategies

11. **Help participants tell their stories.** Adults like to tell stories. Turn this desire into learning and growth by letting the stories form part of the course content. You need to create the structure for this important learning to take place. Emphasize mutual problem solving and sharing of prior life knowledge and experiences. Small groups allow adults to tell their stories. Once you get them started, it is hard to get them to stop. Hearing stories is an ancient means of passing on wisdom. It works. Participants have the opportunity to learn how others solve problems the participants now face or resources that helped. Expand your instruction by letting participants share their valuable knowledge.

12. MAKE IT FUNNY, MAKE IT FUN. Adults should laugh and enjoy themselves, so provide opportunities for playfulness. Use and promote humor that facilitates learning, is in good taste, is appropriate to the task, and matches participant values. Encourage surprise, serendipity, and fun in the learning encounter. Fun and laughter create a wonderfully charged atmosphere for learning.

13. USE IMAGINATION AND THE ARTS. Participants should experience creative expression, which fosters positive change. Employ aspects of the arts (visual arts, music, poetry, drama, and so on) that enhance exploration and learning. Through the arts, encourage participants to stretch beyond limits of understanding, knowledge, and skill. The use of music, drama, writing, or visual arts can help adults shift their frame of reference. Ask participants to write poetry, compose a song, draw, or sculpt—it's an invitation to change.

14. BUILD IN RISK TAKING. The instructor should model willingness to change and promote an attitude of risk taking. The instructor should also model acceptance in the classroom that will lead adults to stretch and grow. You can demonstrate before the group the right and wrong way to diaper a baby or respond to an irate parent or handle a toddler's tantrum. Allow the group to critique your skills. When you model taking risks and welcoming comments, participants see that learning is a process, not an end.

15. TAKE TIME TO REFLECT. Make time for silence, quiet reflection, or journaling to integrate new ideas. At certain times restrict distractions and let the participants become inwardly spontaneous. It is often in the stillness of the mind that deep and true change occurs. Be reluctant to fill every blank moment with words or activity. Writing in a journal is a good example of one way you can encourage participants to assimilate what they have heard in the workshop. Rather than just taking notes, ask participants to record their inner thoughts and feelings, as well as their reactions, to the learning experience.

Make instruction safe

Adults need a comfortable, trust-filled learning environment in order to let go of the old and embrace the new. Participants need to drop their guard and relax. That can happen when adults feel accepted and know that their comfort zones will be respected. Participants will take risks when judgment is suspended; only then will they make those necessary, growth-producing mistakes.

Safe strategies include the following:
- Strategy 16—Help participants feel at home
- Strategy 17—Let participants know what to expect
- Strategy 18—Help participants get acquainted
- Strategy 19—Keep time commitments
- Strategy 20—Build trust and openness

Safe strategies

16. HELP PARTICIPANTS FEEL AT HOME. The learning space should help participants feel relaxed and welcome. Pay attention to creature comforts such as seating arrangements, refreshments, comfortable temperature and lighting, and rest rooms. Welcome participants with visual images that reflect the theme of the class. You may be forced to use facilities with less than desirable conditions, but try to make them comfortable. Design spaces for ease of interaction among adults. Give thought to all the senses: sight, hearing, smell, touch, and taste.

17. LET PARTICIPANTS KNOW WHAT TO EXPECT. Provide participants with clear information about the training event: the objectives, agenda, dates and schedule, place, instructors, format, and cost. Solicit their ideas and develop a workable match between planned activities and participants' needs and desires. The participants should be able to discuss and negotiate various aspects of the program to arrive at a workable arrangement.

18. HELP PARTICIPANTS GET ACQUAINTED. Plan get-acquainted activities so participants can become familiar with each other, the topic, and the instructor. Devise a way to get adults actively involved with each other early on, but show sensitivity to participants' comfort zones. The best use of time is to combine topic-related activities with interpersonal connections. Try to build a sense of trust between adults and raise interest in the program.

19. KEEP TIME COMMITMENTS. Instructors should stick to the schedule as agreed or renegotiate it. Balance the schedule equally between the need to cover the material and the needs of participants. Provide information that

helps participants understand what's at stake when changes are made. Nothing is more irritating and distracting than realizing that the instructor has lost track of the time. Adults fidget, look at watches, and generally suffer in silence. More information gets through when timelines are adhered to.

20. **BUILD TRUST AND OPENNESS.** Participants get close when they discuss their important concerns and help each other solve problems. Employ group-building methods that encourage openness and problem solving. Use small groups, when practical, to provide a catalyst for the free flow of ideas. Closeness and trust help people take risks without fear of judgment. Strike a balance between intimacy and respect for comfort zones. Trust takes time. Plan to keep small groups together over the course of the workshop (unless it seems more important to help participants meet a lot of people). This can build a strong, lasting bond among team members.

A planning sequence

A balance of the four instructor styles can be achieved through a sequence of steps. These steps guide you through a natural progression of planning that helps you use each of the instructor styles and multiple strategies.

Step 1: Plan using the Systematic Instructor Style and strategies. This step helps you establish the basic goals and outline for your instructional program.

Step 2: Plan using the Stimulating Instructor Style and strategies. This step helps you design a program that will meet your instructional goals.

Step 3: Plan using the Spontaneous Instructor Style and strategies. This step helps you make the instruction enjoyable and unique.

Step 4: Plan using the Safe Instructor Style and strategies. This step helps you comfortably draw participants into the experience you have designed.

To properly employ the four instructor styles and ensure the best learning experience for your participants, you must make sure they operate in balance. Balance means that participants benefit equally from each style. They will see the logic of your instruction (systematic), they will be challenged to learn (stimulating), they will experience surprise and humor (spontaneous), and they will feel comfort and trust while learning (safe).

Other Resources from Redleaf Press

The Art of Awareness: How Observation Can Transform Your Teaching
by Deb Curtis and Margie Carter
Do more than watch children—be with children. Covering different aspects of children's lives and how to observe them, as well as tips for gathering and preparing documentation, *The Art of Awareness* is an inspiring look at how to see the children in your care—and how to see what they see.

The Visionary Director: A Handbook for Dreaming, Organizing, and Improving Your Center
by Margie Carter and Deb Curtis
Hear the voices of directors who have used their vision of child care to improve their communities. *The Visionary Director* will inspire directors to look beyond their daily routines and have "bigger dreams for the role their programs can play in reshaping the communities where they reside."

Future Vision, Present Work: Learning from the Culturally Relevant Anti-Bias Leadership Project
by Sharon Cronin, Louise Derman-Sparks, Sharon Henry, Cirecie Olatunji & Stacey York
Based on three leadership groups that performed cross-cultural advocacy work across the country, this book offers timely information addressing anti-bias and cultural relevancy issues for your program.

Theories of Childhood: An Introduction to Dewey, Montessori, Erikson, Piaget, and Vygotsky
by Carol Garhart Mooney
Theories of Childhood examines the work of five groundbreaking educational theorists in relation to early childhood care. Each theorist's ideas are presented to help teachers and students look to the foundations of child care for solutions and guidance in classrooms today.

Training Teachers: A Harvest of Theory and Practice
by Margie Carter and Deb Curtis
Help teachers construct their own knowledge and respect their own learning styles so they can help children do the same. Some of the best ideas in teaching and learning are put into action with these innovative training tools.

Call toll-free 800-423-8309
www.redleafpress.org